"As someone who has been involved ___ and law for over thirty years, I applaud Da ___avert for collecting in one comprehensive work irrefutable evidence of the failings of the current public school system in Kansas. When the legislature challenges the public school system to improve student performance and prepare our youth for college and/or career, the system perpetuates mediocrity, ignores parents and students, and pushes back on legislative reforms that attempt to provide our children with better educational opportunities. This book is a must-read for all Kansas parents and anyone with a passion for education, a thirst for what is truly happening around us in the public education arena, and a desire to implement the reforms that will turn mediocrity into student success."

—Mike O'Neal
Former Speaker of the
Kansas House of Representatives

"If America is to sail confidently into a free and prosperous future, we must fix the education system that acts as an anchor. Will overtaxed and underserved parents demand the necessary changes? Those in Kansas who read this book certainly will, and in doing so they will awaken a nation. Thank you, Trabert and Dorsey, for this genuine public service!"

—Lawrence W. Reed
President Emeritus
Foundation for Economic Education

"It's easy to get complacent about education, especially if you constantly hear, 'Everything is fine, just send money.' This book will shake you out of that complacency reinforced by a constant mantra of 'all is well' from public school officials. You'll demand more honest information, and especially more power for Kansas families: school choice. No more just accepting what the establishment wants you to have."

—Neal P. McCluskey, PhD
Director, Center for Educational Freedom
Cato Institute

"In order to solve a problem, the first thing that must be done by those seeking the truth is to recognize and identify the problem. Two major impediments that basically stop the problem solving are 1) if a 'majority group' believes they already know all the truth, irrespective of all facts and 2) if change comes and it might adversely affect the income of the 'majority group.'

"If either one or both of these are present, the 'majority group' would obviously not be interested in changes. Truth supported by facts is unpleasant for those who think they already know all truth and for whom their income is dependent upon the lie. So be it!

"Trabert and Dorsey have opened a big ol' can of Truth supported by facts. The contents of this book should be pondered and openly discussed by everyone interested in the future of students in Kansas."

—Dr. Steve Abrams
Former State Senator and Chair of the
Kansas Senate Education Committee

"Variety is the spice of life, especially in education. Children vary in passions and aspirations, but you would never know it by looking at what remains as a largely standardized public school system. *Giving Kids a Fight Chance* lays out a compelling case that policymakers should provide meaningful diversity in K–12. One size will fit few; an array of varying schools would allow Kansas families to match the needs of their child with the strengths of diverse schools. Kansas has nothing to lose and much to gain by embracing pluralism by expanding access for all families to a wider universe of schools."

—Matthew Ladner
Executive Editor, ReimaginED

ABOUT KANSAS POLICY INSTITUTE

Kansas Policy Institute is a non-profit research and education organization dedicated to protecting constitutional rights, creating access to better educational opportunities, and helping people keep more of what they earn.

ALSO BY KPI and DAVE TRABERT

*What Was **Really** the Matter with the Kansas Tax Plan:*
The Undoing of a Good Idea

Giving Kids a Fighting Chance with School Choice

Resolving the Social Justice Issue Perpetuated by Kansas Public Schools

DAVE TRABERT
with David Dorsey

Dedication

To George Pearson, Martin Eby, and Gerrit Wormhoudt,
who founded Kansas Policy Institute in 1996,
and with it, the school choice movement in Kansas.

Acknowledgments

The authors and trustees of Kansas Policy Institute are deeply grateful to Colby Sandlian for his support of our Giving Kids a Fighting Chance project and this book.

Colby is a champion of liberty who believes every child should have an equal opportunity to get a high-quality education and achieve the American dream.

He also created the Sandlian Center for Entrepreneurial Government at Kansas Policy Institute in 2018 to help citizens and elected officials explore possible solutions to the many economic challenges facing Kansas. The Sandlian Center provides case studies of successful efforts to reduce costs and offers original research and assistance to state and local elected officials so they can reduce taxes.

We also gratefully acknowledge support from the Garvey Kansas Foundation and John Garvey, in honor of his educational entrepreneur parents, Jean and Willard Garvey, and his grandparents, Olive and Ray Garvey.

Finally, our thanks to Dara Ekanger (www.edityourwork.com) for her editorial polishing, Charles King (www.ckmm.com) for his expert page design and layout, and On the Lake Creative Services (www.onthelakecreative.com) for graphics and cover art.

Contents

(continued)

Foreword

If a picture paints a thousand words, then *Giving Kids a Fighting Chance with School Choice* creates a disturbingly large mural.

At first glance, the book is an in-depth examination of the sclerotic educational bureaucracy in Kansas and its accompanying lack of achievement, its demographic and racial injustice, its over-reliance on funding as a catch-all solution, and its overlapping and counter-productive governmental boards and interests.

But it is much more than that. The sad reality is that a similar book could be written about every state in the union. If you find yourself asking, "Why should I read such a detailed analysis of the Kansas educational bureaucracy?" the answer is that you can probably just swap out the names with the attendant people, places, and institutions from your state and get the same story.

Let me be clear from the outset of this foreword that a discussion of the deleterious effects of *bureaucracy* is not a criticism of *educators*. It's not. The authors could not be more clear in making that known, and they are right to do so. Those looking to improve the working conditions of teachers should lock arms with those casting a critical eye toward the education system's bureaucracy. We must understand the origins and depths of the bureaucracy managing American education to stem the tide of inane and often insane regulations that make it impossible to ensure that students achieve mastery rather than merely completing 180 days in a classroom every year. That is good for students, sure, but it is also good for teachers, who are on the receiving end of those requirements and directives.

They say that those who fail to understand history are doomed to repeat it, and those who understand history are doomed to stand by and watch while they do. But as futile as it may be to look backwards for lessons in a system that always seems to be on the search for the next big thing, for us to truly understand the nature and history of the education bureaucracy in America we have to go back to the mid-1800s and learn about the theories of Adolphe Quetelet, Francis Galton, Frederick Taylor, Horace Mann, and James Blaine. We then have to understand how in the late 1800s and early

1900s, the Carnegie Foundation and the Committee of Ten baked those theories into what has become an ossified, overly bureaucratic education system.

Adolphe Quetelet was a Belgian astronomer, sociologist, and mathematician who greatly influenced social science methodology. He obsessed over the statistical idea of the mythical "Average Man" and believed that the average was the ideal and deviation in either direction was an error. He believed that the greatest historical figures were the nearest approximation to the perfect average man. In his day, he was hailed as a genius and his theories were used by Karl Marx, who argued that the proof of the Average Man demonstrated the existence of historical determinism, as we cannot escape the inexorable realities of statistics.

Francis Galton, a wealthy aristocrat from England, took Quetelet's theories to the next level. He believed that a strong social caste system was far superior to any other democratizing institution, and he used Quetelet's theories to prove his concept. If Quetelet thought the average was the ideal, Galton thought that the average was mediocre. He went about categorizing humanity into 14 different groups—from "Eminent" to "Mediocre" to "Imbecile"—and claimed that everyone's categorization was consistent across multiple measures like intelligence and athletic ability. He argued that better functioning societies would be built around these principles. The application of his theories is described in a term he coined that lives on to this day: eugenics.

Unfortunately, these theories crossed the Atlantic Ocean. One of the devotees of both Quetelet and Galton was an American engineer named Fredrick Taylor. He developed the philosophies of human classification into a system termed Scientific Management. His focus was efficiency and his motto was, "In the past man was first, in the future the system must be first." He believed that standardized, rigorous management, guided by experimentation and observation, could put everyone in society to work advancing the goals of the community. What those goals were, or how they should be determined, remained a sticking point.

What does all this have to do with education? Think about this. When Quetelet was perfecting his ideas of average, Horace Mann was creating the notion of a "common school" that all children were required to attend. When Galton was promoting his idea of categorization, James Blaine was going around promoting laws that would elevate Protestants in education over Catholics. And when Taylor was creating his scientific theory that led to the factory whistle, the Committee of Ten and the Carnegie Foundation were developing ideas that standardized the delivery of all of K–12 education.

The Committee of Ten was established in 1892, and it was made up of the presidents of the leading educational institutions of the time (like Harvard and Vassar). They convened to take Taylor's idea of an efficient factory and create an efficient school. Instead of the factory whistle letting workers know when it was time to quit, it would be the school bell that would let children know when class was over.

Their goal was to standardize everything they could, from the number of years each child would be in school to what was taught in class. According to the committee's official report, they voted unanimously to ensure that "every subject which is taught at all in a secondary school should be taught in the same way and to the same extent to every pupil so long as he pursues it, no matter what the probable destination of the pupil may be, or at what point his education is to cease."

Add to this the development of the Carnegie Unit—the notion that a standardized measure of high school units (seat time) were required to get into college—and you have the final brushstroke in the development of the bureaucratic picture we have today in Kansas and every other state.

Now we can return to the book at hand with a new eye.

Should we be surprised to see a bureaucracy wedded to obfuscating the truth about achievement and routinely painting a much rosier picture about student performance than is actually true? The authors ably dispatch these comforting myths. Despite the claims that Kansas is ahead of the country on achievement, the authors show that only 20 percent of high school students are on track in math and that achievement in Kansas actually declines as a student moves from grade to grade. They point out that the situation is much worse for kids in urban areas and that the achievement gap is far too wide. The authors ask the question whether the current levels of achievement are acceptable. We should too, not just about Kansas but about all K–12 schools in general, whether they are traditional public, charter, private, or online.

The book also discusses at length how much money has been spent on K–12 education in Kansas, noting the court cases that have required hundreds of millions of more dollars to be added to the system. They detail at length that the money hasn't been spent wisely and that anyone who promotes educational options is roundly criticized for "taking money away from the system." It reminded me of the time I once visited Kansas in the early 2000s. A well-known state senator who supported educational choice had arranged a visit to meet with the governor to discuss a proposal to both increase funding and enact a school choice program. I thought it could be a win-win.

I was wrong.

I will never forget the governor's hostility towards choice and insistence on more money as the only solution. It taught me a lesson I will never forget, namely that the bureaucracy in American education exists to preserve its power and money.

Ultimately, the saddest and scariest part of the book is the picture it paints about how the various governmental institutions—the courts, the state board of education, local school boards—seemingly do everything possible to maintain the status quo. Example after example is given about how the educational bureaucracy distracts from the truth about achievement, diverts attention away from whether taxpayer funds are spent effectively or efficiently, and deters any efforts to give parents greater educational options.

As Milton Friedman said in *Free To Choose*, "As the scope and role of government expands—whether by covering a larger area and population or by performing a side variety of functions—the connection between the people governed and the people governing becomes attenuated." Put more simply, as government grows, bureaucracy gets stronger, and the power of people gets weaker.

Trabert and Dorsey are not without solutions. The path forward that they recommend is three-fold.

First, give real power back to parents through greater choice of public, private, or charter schools. It is much more important *that* a child be educated than *where* a child is educated. Second, education needs to be truly accountable—financially, democratically, and educationally. To paraphrase a former Indiana governor, Mitch Daniels, if you are not keeping score then you are just practicing. And third, transparency is a necessary requirement for taxpayers, policymakers, and parents. Without it, no one really knows what is going on.

Ultimately, the painting that we are looking at in Kansas and in America right now is more of a Hieronymus Bosch-like dystopian nightmare. This book can only help the good folks of the Sunflower State—and all of us—pick up a new brush and paint a different picture, one that prominently features more powerful parents and draws a new portrait of transparency and accountability.

—Robert C. Enlow
President & CEO of EdChoice, Inc.,
formerly known as the
Milton and Rose D. Friedman Foundation

Introduction

Public school officials all across the nation enthusiastically declare their devotion to ending racism and discrimination. But like politicians whose actions belie their campaign promises, many of them demonstrate that their sincerity is circumstantial at best by perpetuating educational discrimination.

We document examples of Kansas public school officials prolonging race-based and income-based educational discrimination throughout this book.

The Diversity and Equity Mission Statement of the Shawnee Mission School District in Kansas says the district maintains an educational environment that is free of discrimination.[1] Still, White high school students are five times more likely to be on track for college and career in math than Black students.[2] Income-based educational discrimination is also prevalent in Shawnee Mission. Students who are not from low-income families are four times more likely to be on track in math than low-income students.[3]

Similar achievement gaps exist across Kansas, and education officials defy legislative efforts to address the issue.

The legislature provided about $5 billion of incremental funding since 2005, targeted to help students considered academically and financially at-risk.[4] But a 2015 investigation by Kansas Policy Institute determined that the money wasn't being spent exclusively on at-risk students.[5] A 2019 Legislative Post Audit report had similar results.[6] In one finding, the report says, "In our sample of 20 districts, most at-risk spending was used for teachers and programs for all students and did not appear to specifically address at-risk students as required by state law."

Readers will find other examples of education officials openly defying state law and policy designed to close achievement gaps later in this book. Taken collectively, we conclude that parents cannot count on the public education system to close achievement gaps and improve stubbornly low outcomes for all students.

The Kansas Association of School Boards (KASB) publishes reports that lead parents and legislators to believe that achievement is quite high. Their *Comparing Kansas 2019* report declares, "Kansas Still Ranked 9th in Student Outcomes," even though Kansas didn't have a single ranking in the top ten on any measurable achievement for any demographic cohort.[7]

On the most recent National Assessment of Educational Progress (NAEP) from 2019, Kansas's best ranking is #19 for fourth-grade math proficiency of students who are not low-income. But even rankings can be deceptive. Table 1 shows that Kansas is ranked #20 for math proficiency of low-income students, which may not sound "bad." But only 20% of those students are proficient, and few parents would call that "good."

The ACT exam doesn't provide income-based comparisons, but on its race-based comparisons, the three race-based cohorts that account for the vast majority of Kansas students are each ranked in the low thirties among the fifty states.

Table 1: 2019 NAEP Results		
	Low-Income Students	
Grade Level / Subject	Percent Proficient	National Rank
4th-Grade Reading	20%	#34
4th-Grade Math	25%	#29
8th-Grade Reading	19%	#26
8th-Grade Math	20%	#20
	Not Low-Income Students	
Grade Level / Subject	Percent Proficient	National Rank
4th-Grade Reading	48%	#30
4th-Grade Math	57%	#19
8th-Grade Reading	44%	#25
8th-Grade Math	46%	#29
2021 ACT		
Student Group	% College-Ready	Score Rank
White students	25%	#33
Hispanic students	9%	#34
Black students	5%	#33

And just like on the NAEP, there are significant achievement gaps in college readiness. Of the Kansas graduates who took the 2021 ACT, 25% of White students are college-ready in English, reading, math, and science.

Just 9% of Hispanic students are college-ready, and only 5% of Black students are college-ready.

These achievement gaps have existed for decades.

Students in grades three through eight and the tenth grade take the Kansas State Department of Education (KSDE) state assessment each year (except 2020 was skipped due to the COVID pandemic).

The 2021 results show White high school students are three times more likely to be on track for college and career in math than Black students; the same gap exists between low-income students and their more affluent classmates.[8]

In *Giving Kids a Fighting Chance*—a documentary about Florida's remarkable student achievement gains—former Governor Jeb Bush talks about race- and income-based achievement gaps. Bush hits the urgency of the issue right off the top:

> This is the civil rights issue of our time, it's the economic issue of our time, and it's the social justice issue of our time. Political leaders need to get off the mat and start advocating for meaningful reform, so that there's rising student achievement, so that dreams can come true.[9]

Under his stewardship, reading proficiency for Florida's low-income kids has gone from one of the worst in the nation to one of the best (#1 in fourth grade and #5 in eighth grade).[10] Bush and his team credit the turnaround to a combination of choice, transparency, and accountability, which Kansas public officials strongly oppose.

The problem is not money, teachers, or students. It's a management problem, and management has made it clear that accountability measures are unwelcome, whether in state law or policy. The education governance system outlined in the Kansas Constitution is also a barrier to improvement. That's why educational choice is necessary to get students the education they need to succeed in life.

States with robust choice options have seen remarkable improvement relative to other states, both for the students who take advantage of choice and those who remain in the public school system. Choice breaks the public school monopoly, and that compels public school officials to take action. They must reallocate resources to improve outcomes, or students will take their funding elsewhere.

But that's not all. Employers need workers who have the technical and critical thinking skills required to compete in a global economy, regardless of industry. The Kansas Chamber of Commerce's Vision 2025 statement says,

> Private employment growth in Kansas has struggled in recent years. Technological changes are driving the economy in new directions during the last ten years. The "Internet of Things" is changing how businesses operate—how we heat our offices and factories, organize our production lines, and how and where our employees do their work. Technology is shifting the skills the private sector needs and creating a talent gap in our workforce.[11]

Cybersecurity is one of those new directions with enormous potential for the state to embrace and prepare for this industry's burgeoning demands. A 2020 report by the economic development entity EnterpriseKC said there were over half a million unfilled cybersecurity jobs across the nation, with average entry-level salaries exceeding $90,000 per year. *Fortune Magazine* estimated the cybersecurity industry would grow to more than $270 billion by 2027.[12]

Instead of continually proving Einstein's definition of insanity by attempting to entice companies with subsidies, the State of Kansas could create a significant competitive advantage in this burgeoning field. But opportunities like these will remain beyond the state's grasp if major impediments like low student achievement remain unaddressed.

Students and communities can no longer wait for the public school system to come around. The evidence throughout this book demonstrates that parents must demand robust school choice legislation to give kids a fighting chance.

The depth of the student achievement problem is explored further in Chapter 1. Chapter 2 shares multiple examples of education officials consciously distorting the truth to make student achievement appear higher.

The Kansas State Department of Education and the State Board of Education also are implementing new rules, regulations, and evaluation processes that de-emphasize academic achievement in favor of social-emotional learning. We review those actions in Chapter 3.

Chapter 4 exposes instances of education officials ignoring state laws and policies intended to improve outcomes and close achievement gaps. We demonstrate in Chapter 5 how the state's education governance system stands in the way of better results and proposes an amendment to the Kansas Constitution.

In Chapter 6, we recount the courageous actions taken by the Florida Legislature that produced remarkable achievement gains and discuss specific steps that the Kansas Legislature can take.

Finally, Chapter 7 gives readers many options to get involved and asks them to decide which path they will take. Will parents and the business community collectively compel the legislature and the governor to implement the choice, transparency, and accountability actions needed? Or will they decide that their involvement isn't necessary because the current abysmal achievement levels are acceptable?

Chapter 1—Educational Discrimination and Persistently Low Student Achievement

In Hans Christian Andersen's *The Emperor's New Clothes*, two swindlers arrive at the capital city of an emperor who spends lavishly on clothing at the expense of everything else. Posing as weavers, they offer to supply him with magnificent clothes that are invisible to those who are stupid or incompetent. The emperor hires them, and they set up looms and go to work. A succession of officials and then the emperor himself visit them to check their progress. Each sees that the looms are empty but pretends otherwise to avoid being thought a fool. Finally, the weavers report that the emperor's suit is ready. They mime dressing him, and he sets off in a procession before the city. The townsfolk uncomfortably go along with the pretense, not wanting to appear inept or stupid, until a child blurts out that the emperor is naked. The people then realize that they have been duped. Although startled, the emperor continues the procession, walking more proudly than ever.[13]

The Emperor's New Clothes is a good analogy for discussing student achievement in Kansas. School superintendents, state officials, and local school board members have the data that show achievement is embarrassingly low, but you won't hear them acknowledge the facts. Instead, they point to rising graduation rates and speak in generalities.

For example, the Special Committee on Education asked the department of education to address student achievement at a hearing on November 30, 2021. Their full description follows:

Using the Kansas Assessment Program (KAP) in English Language Arts (ELA), Math and Science, performance was on a decline from 2015 to 2018 and began to level off in 2019. It was our hopes [sic] to see improvement going into 2020, but assessments were not given due to the COVID-19 pandemic. Performance in 2021 saw a decline, much more than any other year prior, which is trending nationally due to the effects that the COVID-19 pandemic had on schools, communities and students.

In addition to KAP performance, student performance on ACT saw an overall state decline, predominately due to the state funding for all students to take the ACT. In the first year of the state paying for each student to have free access to the exam, state-wide participation increased from 72% to 82%. This was the ultimate goal of the legislation, and a new baseline in ACT performance will need to be set once Kansas maintains a consistent level of students taking the exam.[14]

Nothing in the testimony told legislators that achievement was at any particular level.

There is the occasional general acknowledgment that improvement is needed in other public statements, but the overall impression given to the public is that students are doing pretty well.

The Kansas Department of Education's website declares, "Kansas leads the world in the success of each student."[15] The department conducted a fifty-city "Kansans Can Success Tour" in 2021 that felt like high school pep rallies, with the announcement of record-setting high school graduation rates ushered in with great fanfare.

But as the late great Walter Williams said, "It's grossly dishonest for the education establishment and politicians to boast about unprecedented graduation rates when the high school diplomas, for the most part, do not represent academic achievement. At best, they certify attendance."[16]

The Kansas Department of Education gave out sixty-five Gold Awards and twenty-six Silver Awards to districts with high school graduation rates at or above 93%.[17] But how many school districts do you think received Gold or Silver Awards for Academic Preparedness? **Just one**—Unified School District (USD) 207 on the military base at Fort Leavenworth.

The current iteration of the state assessment began in 2015 and scores the results in one of four levels. Figure 1 shows the definitions as explained to legislators when the new assessment was introduced.

Level 1 is below grade level with a limited understanding of subject material. Students in Level 2 have a basic understanding of the material and are considered at grade level but not on track for college and career. Levels 3 and 4 are on track for college and career; students in Level 3 have an effective knowledge of the material, and those in Level 4 have an excellent understanding of the material. The state board of education in January 2016 adopted a definition of a successful high school graduate as having "the academic preparation to be successful . . . without the need for remediation." Since Level 2 is not on track for college and career, those students, by definition, need some degree of remediation.

Fig. 1: KSDE State Assessment

Performance Levels

Kansas Assessment Performance Levels

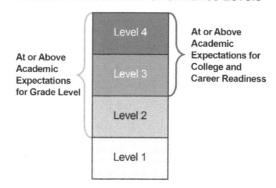

Students in grades three through eight and ten take the state assessment test. All references to high school results reflect the tenth-grade outcomes.

The juxtaposition of graduation rates and state assessment performance for high school students in Kansas illustrates Walter Williams's characterization of high school graduation rates as grossly dishonest.

In math, 47% of high school students are below grade level, and only 20% are on track for college and career. The results in English language arts are 35% and 26%, respectively.

The state assessment results show there are more high school students below grade level than are on track for college and career, but KDSE celebrates an 88% graduation rate. High school diplomas are indeed nothing more than attendance certificates for many students.

And like the townspeople who observed the emperor parading

naked down the street, superintendents and school board members sit by silently as diplomas are awarded to students who are below grade level.

This harsh reality was voiced at a meeting of the Public Policy & Advocacy Committee of the Overland Park Chamber of Commerce in 2019. The high school results for that year shown in Table 2 reflect 41% are below grade level in math, and Table 3 shows a third of students below grade level in English language arts.

Several committee members expressed strong disagreement about students getting a diploma even though they are below grade level. One member questioned the speaker's motives and stormed out of the room.

But the two school superintendents in attendance said nothing. Olathe Superintendent John Allison and Shawnee Mission Superintendent Michael Fulton offered no rebuttal, as they couldn't dispute the state assessment results. Olathe had 31% below grade level in math, and 27% were below grade level in ELA. The results in Shawnee Mission were 35% and 26%, respectively. Further discussion would only underscore the disparity between their public statements and reality.[18]

Table 2: High School Math			
District	Below Grade Level	At Grade Level, Needs Remedial Training	On Track for College & Career
State average	41%	34%	25%
Shawnee Mission	35%	32%	33%
Olathe	31%	32%	37%
Blue Valley	21%	30%	49%
Source: KSDE; 2019 state assessment			

Table 3: High School ELA			
Year	Below Grade Level	At Grade Level, Needs Remedial Training	On Track for College & Career
State average	34%	37%	29%
Shawnee Mission	26%	36%	38%
Olathe	27%	35%	38%
Blue Valley	21%	34%	45%
Source: KSDE; 2019 state assessment			

Shawnee Mission, Olathe, and Blue Valley are the three largest districts in Johnson County, adjacent to Kansas City, Missouri. Johnson County schools are often touted as among the best in Kansas and the nation, but that reputation is more driven by marketing hype and demographics than achievement.

The race-based and income-based achievement gaps discussed in the Introduction are significant in Johnson County, the most affluent county in Kansas. Eligibility for free or reduced lunch is the dividing line between low-income and the more affluent students in education. Statewide, 42% of headcount enrollment is low-income students. But only 19% of students in Johnson County qualify for free or reduced lunch.[19]

A simple grade-point average exercise demonstrates the advantage this gives Johnson County schools. For simplicity, let's say that all low-income students in Kansas and Johnson County get a D (worth 1 point on a 4-point GPA scale), and all other students get a B. The state average GPA would be 2.1 (42% of students with a D and 58% with a B), but Johnson County would have a 2.5 GPA. Students of both income categories have the same grades, but Johnson County appears to have better results because fewer students are low-income. In other words, there is no achievement difference, just demographic disparity.

The Blue Valley School District has the most significant advantage in Johnson County, with low-income students comprising less than 8% of enrollment. Its GPA in the above example would be 2.8, and that may sound good. But a quarter of Blue Valley high school students were below grade level in math on the 2021 state assessment, and less than half were on track for college and career. The district's marketing hype focuses on an artificially inflated GPA, obscuring disappointing student achievement that matters to parents.

Achievement falls despite significant funding increases
Many education officials equate higher funding with student achievement, and they want parents to believe that higher spending is required to improve outcomes. For example, the Kansas Association of School Boards (KASB) published *Comparing Kansas 2019*. They say that the only eight states that outperformed Kansas

"have higher total revenue per pupil than Kansas, meaning they all spend more on average per student than Kansas."[20]

But their claim is very deceptive. KASB uses a proprietary methodology in which actual achievement on the ACT and the National Assessment of Educational Progress (NAEP) counts for just one-third of a state's score. KASB uses scores for some students on NAEP more than once.[21]

On the most recent National Assessment of Educational Progress from 2019, Kansas's best ranking is #19 for fourth-grade math proficiency of students who are not low-income. The rest of the NAEP rankings are in the twenties and thirties.

ACT breaks out scores by race, not income levels. The 2021 results show White students in Kansas are ranked 33rd best among White students in the fifty states; Hispanic students are 40th nationally; and Black students are ranked 35th.

Overall, Kansas is a little below average in the nation with, at best, mediocre results.

Fig. 2: Spending Far Outpaces Inflation, NAEP Proficiency is Lower

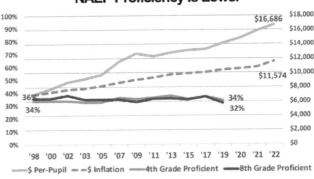

Source: Nation's Report Card (NAEP); Kansas Dept. of Education

As seen in Figure 2, only about a third of students tested are reading proficiently on the NAEP. Proficiency declined a bit since 1998, but actual per-student spending increased much faster than inflation.

The complete 2019 NAEP results are available in Appendix A.

Money matters, of course, but only if properly used.

Dr. Eric Hanushek writes, "[T]he outcomes observed over the past half-century—no matter how massaged—do not suggest that just throwing money at schools is likely to be a policy that solves the significant U.S. schooling problems seen in the levels and distribution of outcomes. We really cannot get around the necessity of focusing on how money is spent on schools."[22]

A large body of research emphasizes the outsized role that teachers play in preparing students to be successful in life. *In Teacher Quality: Understanding the Effectiveness of Teacher Attributes*, author Jennifer Rice King references research by Steven Rivkin, Eric Hanushek, and John Kain. King writes, "Their research identifies teacher quality as the most important school-related factor influencing student achievement. They conclude from their analysis of 400,000 students in 3,000 schools that, while school quality is an important determinant of student achievement, the most important predictor is teacher quality."[23]

Attracting and retaining effective teachers matters a great deal. Superintendents, school board members, and their lobbyists routinely cite low teacher pay as a problem in Kansas, which they use to justify their demands for more money. But the problem is not a lack of funding; instead, it's how the education bureaucracy has chosen to spend money.

Inflation-adjusted per-student spending increased 52% in Kansas between 1992 and 2019, but the average teacher salary *declined* by 9%. Local school boards had a lot more money to spend, but they decided to spend it on other things, like hiring many more employees who aren't teachers. Over the same period, headcount enrollment increased by 12% in Kansas; school boards hired 25% more teachers, but all other school staff jumped by 56%.[24]

Given how local school boards and administrators have chosen to spend money, it is not surprising that ACT results are also declining. College readiness in English, reading, math, and science was 24% in 2002. It peaked at 32% in 2015 but declined steadily to just 21% for Kansas graduates who took the 2021 ACT. And college readiness on the ACT is not a high bar. ACT defines college readiness as having a 75% chance or better of getting a "C" or higher on an entry-level course or a 50% chance of getting a "B" or higher.[25]

The department of education attributes part of the decline to more students taking the test, and the research validates their position. Since the legislature started paying the fee, participation increased from the low 70s to 79% in 2021.

Deputy Commissioner Brad Neuenswander told legislators that ACT scores would continue to decline until participation is about 95%, and there was no accompanying sense of urgency.[26] Think about that: college readiness could dip into the teens, and no alarm bells are going off.

A history of ACT college readiness is in Appendix B.

Kansas is #38 in bang for the educational buck
To fairly compare state spending and achievement, Kansas Policy Institute uses a methodology first developed by Dr. Benjamin Scafidi, director of the Education Economics Center at Kennesaw State University.[27]

Scafidi calculated a composite score for each state using the eight main NAEP measurements—fourth-grade and eighth-grade reading and math for low-income students and those who are not low-income. Spending per student for each state is adjusted for the cost of living because a dollar spent in Kansas buys a lot more than a dollar spent in New York or California. Scafidi uses the Missouri Economic Research and Information Center (MERIC) for the cost of living (COL) adjustments.[28]

Each state's relative productivity—what some might call "bang for the buck"—can be measured by dividing the NAEP composite score into per-student spending to find the cost per point scored.

Consider the productivity analysis that uses spending reported by the U.S. Census for the 2019 school year and the 2019 NAEP scores.[29] With COL-adjusted expenditures at $16,661 per student and a 251 NAEP composite, Kansas spends $66 per NAEP point.[30] That's worse than the national average of $59 per point and places Kansas at #38 on the productivity bang-for-the-buck ranking.

Hawaii had the best productivity at $36 per NAEP point, followed closely by Idaho, Utah, Arizona, and Florida. New York had the lowest productivity at $82 per NAEP point; Pennsylvania, New Jersey, Illinois, and Wyoming were the next worst.

A straight comparison of NAEP scores and per-student spending from 2019 shows no correlation. For example, six states had the exact composite score of the eight primary NAEP categories. But, adjusting per-student spending for the cost of living, spending for those states ranged from as little as $11,000 per student in North Carolina to more than $19,000 in Illinois.

Appendix C lists the results for all fifty states.

One-third below grade level on the state assessment test
States change their assessment tests periodically, so historical performance is more limited than NAEP and ACT.

In both subjects—math and English language arts—achievement declined over the last five years. (There was no test in 2020 because Gov. Kelly closed schools during the COVID pandemic.)

Table 4 shows a third of students tested are below grade level in math, and 38% are at grade level but need some degree of remedial training; only about a quarter of students are on track for college and career. Roughly a third of students are in each category for English language arts, as shown in Table 5. Department of education officials largely blame the most recent declines on COVID, but the decision to deny in-person learning for a large portion of the year for most students was a choice made by local school boards.

Table 4: All Students/All Grades - Math			
Year	Below Grade Level	At Grade Level, Needs Remedial Training	On Track for College & Career
2016	27%	38%	34%
2017	28%	38%	33%
2018	29%	38%	33%
2019	28%	39%	33%
2021	34%	38%	28%
Source: KSDE; totals <100% due to students not tested			

Table 5: All Students/All Grades - ELA			
Year	Below Grade Level	At Grade Level, Needs Remedial Training	On Track for College & Career
2016	24%	35%	40%
2017	27%	34%	37%
2018	29%	34%	37%
2019	29%	34%	37%
2021	30%	35%	35%
Source: KSDE; totals <100% due to students not tested			

Parents asked school board members to explain how they determined that the perceived health benefits of keeping students at home outweighed the known educational losses and emotional consequences. The only replies were word salads or deer-in-the-headlight stares. School boards may have been succumbing to the demands of adults who work in schools, but they cannot "show their work" to prove their decisions were in the best overall interests of students.

However, evidence shows COVID-driven restrictions on in-person learning and mask mandates were detrimental to academic progress and created mental health challenges.

A Brookings analysis found significant drops in math and reading scores and widening educational discrimination gaps.

Average fall 2021 math test scores in grades 3-8 were 0.20-0.27 standard deviations (SDs) lower relative to same-grade peers in fall 2019, while reading test scores were 0.09-0.18 SDs lower. This is a sizable drop. For context, the math drops are significantly larger than estimated impacts from other large-scale school disruptions, such as after Hurricane Katrina—math scores dropped 0.17 SDs in one year for New Orleans evacuees.

Even more concerning, test-score gaps between students in low-poverty and high-poverty elementary schools grew by approximately 20% in math (corresponding to 0.20 SDs) and 15% in reading (0.13 SDs), primarily during the 2020–21 school year. Further, achievement tended to drop more between fall 2020 and 2021 than between fall 2019 and 2020 (both overall and differentially by school poverty), indicating that disruptions to learning have continued to negatively impact students well past the initial hits following the spring 2020 school closures.[31]

Another study of the nation's top five hundred school districts indicates that masking children in school had the opposite effect that proponents hoped. On average, children in masked schools experienced 4 times the number of disrupted learning days as those in mask-optional districts, and they also had 2.5 times higher case rates of COVID-19 during the same period.[32]

More high school students are below grade level than on track for college and career

The high school results are far worse than the averages shown in Tables 4 and 5.

- Only 20% of high school students are on track for college and career in math; 47% are below grade level.
- Just a quarter of high school students are on track in English language arts, and 35% are below grade level.

Those are the statewide averages; proficiency is much lower in urban areas. (The Kansas Department of Education equates "on track for college and career" with proficiency, having told the U.S. Department of Education that Levels 3 and 4 are proficient but not Levels 1 and 2.)[33]

In Wichita, the state's largest district, 68% of high school students are below grade level in math, and only 10% are proficient. Kansas City, Kansas, has 71% below grade level, and only 7% are proficient. The results in Topeka are 64% and 11%, respectively.

But it is not just an urban issue; the problem also exists in the leafy, more affluent suburbs.

- A quarter of the more affluent high school students in Blue Valley (the state's wealthiest district) are below grade level in math, and less than half are proficient.
- A third of students are below grade level in the Auburn-Washburn district near Topeka, and just a quarter are proficient in math.
- The Andover district, where some of the more affluent families near Wichita send their children, has 20% below grade level in math, and only about a third are proficient.

Cities that are home to the state's six universities also have achievement challenges, as seen in Table 6. In fact, except for Hays, home to Fort Hays State University, those cities have more high school students below grade level in math than are on track for college and career.

Lawrence, home to the University of Kansas, has 42% below grade level, and 26% are proficient. In Kansas State University's hometown of Manhattan, 38% are below grade level, and only 30% are proficient. Wichita, home to Wichita State University, is the worst; 68% are below grade level, and just 10% are proficient.

Table 6: All Students/High School - Math			
District	Below Grade Level	At Grade Level, Needs Remedial Training	On Track for College & Career
Lawrence	42%	32%	26%
Manhattan	38%	32%	30%
Wichita	68%	22%	10%
Emporia	49%	33%	18%
Pittsburg	45%	27%	29%
Hays	31%	37%	32%
State Average	47%	33%	20%
Source: KSDE			

Some 49% of students in the hometown of Emporia State University are below grade level in math, and only 18% are proficient. In Pittsburg, home to Pittsburg State University, the results are 45% and 29%, respectively.

Appendix D has state assessment results for Kansas's twenty-five largest public school districts.

Achievement declines as students move from one grade to the next
Achievement levels are typically at the lowest in high school, and the slide begins very early.

Figure 3 shows that 34% of fifth graders were proficient in English language arts in 2016. The following year those students were in the sixth grade, and proficiency fell to 32%. Proficiency continued declining in seventh grade and eighth grade, dropping to 28% and 26%, respectively, and then fell to 20% in the tenth grade.

Those results are for all students. Outcomes also progressively decline for the income-based cohorts, but the decline is more severe for low-income students. Their proficiency levels drop by about two-thirds between fifth grade and tenth grade, whereas students who are not low-income lose about half.

Fig. 3: Proficiency Declines
As Students Move From One Grade to the Next

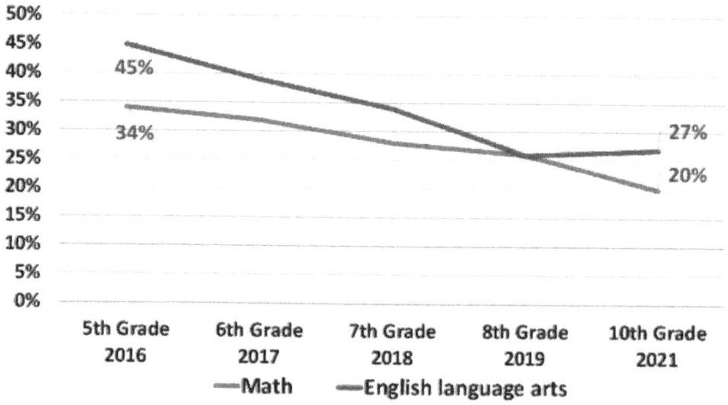

Source: KSDE, Kansas Report Card. Percent of students on track for college and career.

These trends indicate that students cannot keep up as school-work becomes more challenging, likely because they aren't getting an adequate knowledge base in the early years. The trends also indicate that achievement is more likely to decline than improve between tenth grade—the last year tested—and graduation.

Race-based and income-based educational discrimination
Across Kansas, local school boards and administrators effusively declare their devotion to equality and eliminating discrimination. But persistent achievement gaps between racial groups and income levels reveal their intentions to be circumstantial at best.

The 2021 state assessment results in Table 7 show White students in Kansas are three times more likely to be on track for college and career (proficient) than Black students in math and more than twice as likely as Hispanic students. Conversely, Black students are three times more likely to be below grade level, and Hispanic students are more than twice as likely.

Students who are not from low-income families are more than twice as likely to be proficient in math as low-income students, and low-income kids are twice as likely to be below grade level than their more affluent peers.

English language arts results reflect similar gaps.

Table 7: Race, Income Achievement Gaps All Grades-Math			
Subject / Cohort	Below Grade Level	At Grade Level, Needs Remedial Training	On Track for College & Career
Race			
White students	27%	39%	34%
Hispanic students	50%	36%	14%
Black students	61%	29%	10%
Income			
Not low-income	25%	38%	37%
Low-income	48%	37%	15%
Source: KSDE, 2021 state assessment			

The results in Table 7 reflect the statewide averages. Table 8 shows that the gaps for individual districts also vary by a factor of two or more across several of the state's larger districts outside major metropolitan areas.

Students who aren't low-income are two to three times more likely to be proficient than low-income students in Hutchinson, Salina, Garden City, and Lawrence. And in most cases, roughly half of low-income students are below grade level.

Income-based educational discrimination is even worse in urban areas.

These examples of educational discrimination on the state assessment test also appear in the ACT college-readiness results.

Table 8: Income-Based Gaps All Grades - Math			
Subject / Cohort	Below Grade Level	At Grade Level, Needs Remedial Training	On Track for College & Career
Hutchinson			
Not low-income	30%	43%	27%
Low-income	53%	37%	10%
Salina			
Not low-income	26%	40%	34%
Low-income	47%	39%	14%
Garden City			
Not low-income	39%	37%	24%
Low-income	52%	36%	12%
Lawrence			
Not low-income	22%	38%	40%
Low-income	53%	33%	14%
Source: KSDE, 2021 state assessment			

Only 5% of 2021 Black graduates who took the ACT are considered college-ready in English, reading, math, and science, and just 9% of Hispanic graduates are. White students are much higher, at 25% college-ready. These gaps have remained relatively steady since 2002, the earliest that this data is readily available.

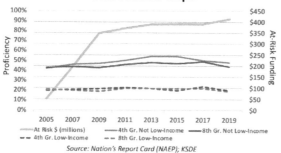

Fig. 4: 8-Fold Increase of At-Risk Funding Little Change in Income-Based Achievement Gaps

Source: *Nation's Report Card (NAEP); KSDE*

The National Assessment of Educational Progress results in Figure 4 also show consistent gaps in reading proficiency since 1998, when Kansas first participated in NAEP. Proficiency for low-income students in fourth grade and eighth grade has hovered around 20% the entire time, while proficiency for students who are not low-income ranged between 40% and 50%.

And the gaps grew wider. In 2005, there was a 22-point gap between the groups in fourth grade and eighth grade. But in 2019, the gap was 28 points in fourth grade (20% vs. 48%) and it was 25 points in eighth grade (19% vs. 44%).

The NAEP raw scores provide an even more disturbing perspective. Ten points on the NAEP are equivalent to a year's worth of learning.[34] The 2019 NAEP raw score for low-income students in fourth-grade reading was 206, but their more affluent peers had a score of 233. That twenty-seven-point difference means the low-income kids are about 2.7 years' worth of learning behind—in the fourth grade!

The gap was 2.3 years in 1998. Low-income students had the same score (206), and the score for those who weren't low-income was 229.

And once again, extra funding had no impact. The Kansas Legislature increased annual funding for at-risk students from about

$50 million in 2005 to $350 million annually in 2009, with subsequent gradual raises to more than $400 million. Over that period, schools received more than $5 billion in cumulative incremental funding to close income-based achievement gaps, but students received no benefit.

It is deplorable that these gaps exist, but even worse, they have remained relatively unchanged for years and largely ignored by local school district officials.

Audits show that the $5 billion in incremental at-risk funding since 2005 is not being spent as intended.[35] A law passed more than twenty years ago requires local school boards to conduct an annual needs assessment of each attendance center; barriers to raising achievement levels must be identified and used to inform the budget process. But an audit of the twenty-five largest districts found only two that examined each school, and none could demonstrate that they identified specific needs and made the appropriate budgetary provisions.[36] Chapter 3 explores both of these situations in greater detail.

Private schools in Kansas have better outcomes than public schools
Students from low-income families and students of color are just as capable of learning as other students. Their low outcomes are not a matter of intelligence but educational environment.

The impact of the educational environment exists in comparing the performance of low-income students in Kansas public schools and low-income kids who attend private schools that take the state assessment test.

Table 9: Low-Income Proficiency All Grades		
District	Math	ELA
Kansas City Diocese	21%	30%
USD 500 Kansas City	7%	13%
Dodge City Diocese	30%	35%
USD 443 Dodge City	14%	16%
Salina Diocese	26%	37%
USD 305 Salina	14%	23%
Topeka Lutheran	38%	43%
USD 501 Topeka	8%	12%
Kansas Public avg.	15%	21%
Source: 2021 State Assessment		

Table 9 compares each of the Catholic dioceses in Kansas and the Topeka-based Lutheran schools with its home-based public school district. In every case, the low-income students in the private school districts have much better outcomes. And in all but one instance—Salina—the private school students are two to three times more likely to be proficient in math and English language arts. Salina's gap isn't as wide, but the Catholic schools still have better performance.

This isn't an exact apples-to-apples comparison; not all of the parochial school systems have a high school in each city, for one thing. But the private schools outperform public schools even at individual grade levels in elementary schools.

The disparity in public and private school performance is crucial in the school choice debate. Tax credit scholarships and some education savings account programs target low-income families, and the Kansas achievement comparison shows that their children have better private opportunities.

Summing it all up

Whether student achievement is "good" is not about all students being at a particular level of achievement. But every Kansan must examine the results and reach their conclusions with this question in mind: *Are the current achievement levels acceptable?*

Those for whom the answer is "yes" will understandably want the public school system to proceed on its current path.

But those who don't believe achievement levels are acceptable must then determine whether school districts will ever attain an adequate achievement level if left to their own devices.

Chapters 2 through 5 will help answer that question.

Chapter 2—Education Officials Won't Tell the Truth about Achievement

Like the weavers in *The Emperor's New Clothes*, the Kansas Department of Education and school district administrators know they aren't honest about achievement levels. They have access to the ACT, NAEP, and state assessment scores outlined in Chapter 1, often at more granular levels than the public-facing data.

To be clear, their characterizations of achievement are not just putting a positive "spin" on results; there are documented cases of officials consciously making statements designed to give a false sense of higher achievement.

In a September 28, 2021, email exchange with Kansas Policy Institute, Deputy Commissioner Brad Neuenswander said, "The Kansas assessment no longer measures grade-level performance."[37] That claim is in direct conflict with the state board of education standards approved in 2015, shown earlier in Figure 1. Levels 2, 3, and 4 are designated as grade level, leaving Level 1 below grade level.

In that same exchange, Neuenswander said performance at Level 2 on the state assessment is on track for college and career: "A student performing at mid-level 2 on the ELA assessment, according to research performed by KU [the University of Kansas] since the original cut scores were set, meets the ACT college readiness benchmark."

At the very least, he admits that not everyone in Level 2 is on track for college and career. But even that doesn't pass muster.

Figure 5 shows the 2019 state assessment results for Math and ELA (when the 2021 graduating class was in the tenth grade). The ELA results show 34% in Level 1, 37% in Level 2, and 28% in Levels 3 and 4 combined.

By the Department of Education's "new math," 65% of high school students would be on track in English language arts and 59% in math. But the 2021 ACT results report that only 21% were college-ready in English, reading, math, and science. ACT College-readiness on individual subjects may be higher, but having only one in five graduates college-ready in all four core subjects is abysmal.

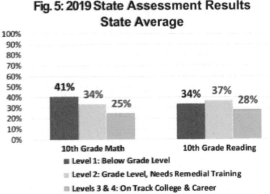

Fig. 5: 2019 State Assessment Results
State Average

The disparity cannot be attributed to COVID, as the same gross inconsistencies existed previously. It also cannot be explained away by variances in standards. The percent of Kansas students considered to be college ready by their ACT scores has been in the twenties for several years. Department of education officials never tried to explain that away as Kansas having higher standards than the ACT. Instead, department officials and the Kansas Association of School Boards attempted to justify the results by demonstrating that public schools were doing well. The logic went like this: "Well, only about 20% of jobs require a college degree, so having 21% college-ready shows schools are doing a good job."

The exchange with Neuenswander was prompted by false claims posted to social media by a local school board member earlier that month. Brandon Parks was running for re-election to the Gardener-Edgerton School Board in Johnson County. His opponent, Jeff Miller, was telling parents the truth about student achievement in the district, prompting Parks to say that students scoring in Level 2 are on track for college and career.[38]

Neuenswander responded to Kansas Policy Institute's request for clarification on September 28, writing, "Level 1 is the only assessment category that defines students as not yet ready for college and career."

But just three days prior, on September 25, Neuenswander told a parent a different story. The parent wrote, "Hey! I'm looking at our district's scores. Please see attached. Would Level 2 be considered on track for college and career?"

Neuenswander replied, "No. Levels 3 and 4 indicates [*sic*] that they are on track for college level work."[39]

The month before, the department of education gave awards to districts for being academically prepared for post-secondary success. The explanation on the department of education website says, "For Kansas to achieve its vision for education in the area of academic preparation, 75% of all students need to score at or above Levels 3 and 4 on state assessments."[40]

Not Level 2, or even part of Level 2; only scores in Levels 3 and 4 count for the award.

The department also told the U.S. Department of Education that only Levels 3 and 4 are considered proficient.

In January 2018, they submitted a plan to the U.S. Department of Education for compliance with the Elementary and Secondary Act. The Academic Achievement section on page 25 says, "Levels 1 and 2 are categorized as not proficient. Levels 3 and 4 are proficient."[41]

It begs credulity for state department of education officials to claim that non-proficient students are academically prepared for college and career.

There is also no evidence that the state board of education modified the cut scores for grade level and proficiency that it approved in 2015. Neuenswander was asked to provide documentation of the board voting to approve any changes in the September 28 email. He did not respond.[42]

Kansas is the Lake Wobegon of education

Garrison Keillor hosted "Prairie Home Companion" on National Public Radio in the 1980s. It was about a fictional city called Lake Wobegon, which Keillor described as a place where "all women are strong, all men are good-looking, and all children are above average."[43]

While Keillor's description is obviously tongue-in-cheek, some education officials would like parents to believe that no school districts are below average. A 1987 study released by Friends of Education, an advocacy group in West Virginia, found that normed tests were skewed to see the overwhelming majority of elementary school students nationwide scored above average.[44]

The study funded by Beckley, West Virginia, physician John Jacob Cannell suggested that "norm-referenced tests—in which students are compared with a group tested in the past, not with other test takers—do not represent an accurate appraisal of academic performance."

In an interview with Education Week, Dr. Cannell said test publishers "want to have good news to sell to superintendents."

In the Kansas version of Lake Wobegon, all students are at or above grade level.

But that's not true, of course. The state assessment level descriptions introduced in 2015 clearly showed that Level 1 was not at grade level (See Figure 1). The department of education has produced no evidence that the state board of education voted to change the cut scores that determined Level 2 as being grade level. The words 'grade level' have been scrubbed from the descriptors now used for each level, but the Kansas Association of School Boards said that Level 2 is grade-level in a report dated July 22, 2022.[45] That report doesn't mention Level 1, but it says Levels 3 and 4 reflect higher performance, so Level 1 is logically below grade level.

The July 22 acknowledgement of what constitutues grade level may indicate that KASB has given up trying to fool people into believing that there is no such thing as grade level on the state assessment. It and and the Department of Education previously worked hard to make people believe that grade level isn't measured on the state assessment (so they don't have to defend having many students below grade level).

Deputy Superintendent Neuenswander said in his September 28, 2021 email, "The Kansas assessment no longer measures grade-level performance."[46]

That claim was repeated on February 10, 2022, by Mark Tallman, associate executive director of advocacy for the Kansas Association of School Boards. Tallman was testifying before the Senate Education Committee, during which he said the achievement of grade level on the state assessment is not defined. Committee Chair Sen. Molly Baumgardner wasn't buying it.

"Mr. Tallman, did I hear you say there are no standards for grade levels?" she asked.

He chose his words carefully in responding: "No, what I'm saying is at least my understanding now is the state reports four benchmark levels. One, two, three, and four. There are descriptors of each of those levels, but there is not one that is referred to as being on grade level. I think people generally colloquially refer to like two and above as being on grade level, and three and above as being college and career-ready, but if you look on the [department of education] website, unless something has changed, those specific [grade level] labels are not attached."

Baumgardner pushed back, asking, "Then what the heck would third-grade reading competency be?"

Tallman didn't have an answer but deflected, saying, "I think that would have to be defined as 'what do you mean by that?' Do you mean Level 2, do you mean Level 3?"

Baumgardner continued her cross-examination: "This is coming from the department of education Kansas Can outcomes. So are you telling me that the state board of education hasn't defined what third-grade reading competency is? Is that what we're supposed to believe?"

Tallman replied, "My understanding is that if you look at their definition . . . they have a definition of what Level 2 means or Level 3 means . . . none of those definitions include the phrase 'grade level.'"[47]

The definitions approved in 2015 by the state board of education unquestionably identified Levels 2, 3, and 4 as being at grade level, leaving Level 1 below grade level. But parents are finally beginning to realize that achievement is lower than they are led to believe, so education officials are trying a different type of deception rather than own it and do right by students.

This attempt to convince Kansans that they aren't seeing what is right before them demonstrates that academically preparing students for college and career is not the primary focus of the public school system. Students and parents have little hope that education officials will resolve a problem that they refuse to admit even exists.

And this is far from being the only example.

State school board president consciously deceives Kansans

On February 11, 2021, the House K–12 Budget Committee heard testimony from state education officials about efforts to overcome severe learning loss related to school districts' handling of the COVID situation. After several presentations, Rep. Brenda Landwehr got to the heart of the issue:

> As I sat here and listened to the report that you provided and read a couple of the pages on the chart that you had up on the screen, I think that you probably need to expand your vocabulary. We hear "have a clear strategic plan"; well, we should have had one of those before now. "Account for every student, reconnect with students who have disengaged from instruction"; I would hope we would have done that before now.
>
> "Develop plans for assessing and analyzing academic and social-emotional needs of each student"; I would hope we would have done that before now. "Prepare the 2021 class for graduation"; that needed to start last summer. "Create and provide academic enrichment and supervised activities that go beyond the traditional school year and daily schedule." "Identify and promote child and adult well-being." "Plan master schedule for 2021 school year." Create innovative practices and environments to address this course correction." "Extending the school years for two years."
>
> Most of these kids have lost almost a year of school. I know the largest district in the State of Kansas was handing out packets; there was no remote instruction. How are those kids even learning?
>
> I'm hearing this talk from a level that's on high from the department of education here, but how does that trickle down to our local school boards into details . . . to know exactly what their plans are? What are . . . have . . . their plans been? What are they currently doing? You know, when you've got parents, and you've got kids that are in tears because they don't know from one day to the next whether they're remote, whether they're in, whether they're going to be able to go to work. If

we go back through your testimony over the last years, we can hear a lot of these same words in there. And it all sounds good, and we get a lot of fluff when we're talked to in this committee, but where's the bullet points of this is exactly what we're going to do? "This is exactly how we're going to do it. This is the agreement that we have gotten from local school boards," because you don't get to tell them what to do.[48]

Landwehr's comments focused on schools' handling of the COVID situation, but her remarks reflect legislators' concerns for more than a decade.

- Legislators or parents raise an issue.
- The bureaucracy prepares a document with perhaps good intentions but few specific actions and follow-ups.
- Nothing of substance changes.
- Rinse and repeat.

Ranchers call this "all hat and no cattle."

Committee Chair Kristey Williams said many legislators share Landwehr's concerns and then posed a question to the president of the state board of education, Jim Porter.

We received a summary of the January 2021 state board of education's actions, updates, and legislative priorities. When I looked at the legislative priorities—they were one and a half pages—I could not find one item on the list where the state board wanted to partner with the legislature to improve achievement. And that concerned me. [You] want to reinstate the high density at-risk [funding] weighting support, follow state statute and move up to funding 92% of special education. [You] oppose infringement of state board responsibility to determine statewide curriculum standards. [You] oppose any reduction of modification to recommendation for funding levels.

For the past three years in this committee, one thing that has been consistent [is] achievement, achievement, achievement,

achievement. And what kind of scares me is that if . . . we need to be partners, we want to be partners. There's not one word of achievement, and in the document for "Navigating Next," there was no word of the state assessment. "The state board authorized Navigating Next." So the state board is not alerting the school districts that there is a state assessment.

So, Jim, I just want to understand, why is achievement missing in this?[49]

Porter answered that achievement is always at the top of the state board's list, although most of their published material does not support his claim. Then he tried to reinforce his deception with a standard bureaucratic non-sequitur maneuver.

Porter referenced a slide in the presentation from a National Assessment of Educational Progress report that shows Kansas has higher state proficiency standards than most states.[50] According to the NAEP mapping study, proficient performance on the Kansas state assessment is higher than what NAEP considers proficient in three of the four cases (i.e., fourth grade reading and math; eighth grade reading and math).

Here is the implication of the NAEP mapping study in a practical example. In 2019, the state assessment showed that 29% of eighth-grade students were proficient in English language arts, and the 2019 NAEP results showed that 32% of Kansas eighth-grade students were proficient in reading. So since Kansas has a higher bar for proficiency in this measurement, it's fair to say that the state assessment result of 29% is likely at or a little above 32% from a national perspective.

But that is not at all what Porter told the committee: "We have set our assessment scores [proficiency levels] significantly higher than many other states because we want that to be a challenge goal. So when you hear that X% of students are performing at proficient or above and we should compare that to, well, typically Florida, you need to see where those rates are."

Porter's response had nothing to do with the question asked by Rep. Williams, and his Florida reference implies that he is either consciously deceptive or horribly misinformed.

States' performance on NAEP is unaffected by state assessment standards. Students in every state take the same NAEP test, and it is fair to compare the results at face value. In fourth-grade reading for low-income students, 28% of Florida students were proficient in 2019, but only 20% of Kansas students were proficient. Porter's reference to Florida is an attempt to dismiss its superior performance as a methodological anomaly.

By the way, it's essential to differentiate between state "standards" and classroom activity. A standard determines what is expected of students to achieve a certain level of performance. For example, the tenth-grade reading standard in Kansas expects students to "cite strong and thorough textual evidence to support analysis of what the text says explicitly as well as inferences drawn from the text."[51]

The department of education determines the appropriate "cut scores" on the state assessment test that coincide with specific definitions of accomplishment such as "proficient"; it is akin to a teacher setting the cut score for an "A" on a test at 90% or higher. In terms of the NAEP mapping study, it would be like NAEP saying 90–100 is proficient, but Kansas uses a scale of 94–100.

However, what occurs in classrooms is an entirely different matter, both in content and accomplishment. One teacher could use Karl Marx's *Communist Manifesto*, while another teacher in the same school might use *The Writings of Thomas Jefferson*. Grading performance in the classroom is another variable; one teacher may require much less of a student to earn a passing grade than another teacher.

Table 10 shows Florida had better outcomes than Kansas on six of the eight primary NAEP measurements in 2019; there was one tie, and Kansas did better by a single percentage point on one measurement (eighth-grade math for low-income students). That is a complete turnaround since 2003 when Kansas did better on six comparisons, there was one tie, and Florida had a single win.[52]

Table 10: NAEP Proficiency 2019		
Grade/Subject	Florida	Kansas
4th-Gr. Reading low-income	28%	20%
4th-Gr. Reading not low-income	52%	48%
8th-Gr. Reading low-income	25%	19%
8th-Gr. Reading not low-income	47%	44%
4th-Gr. Math low-income	38%	25%
4th-Gr. Math not low-income	62%	57%
8th-Gr. Math low-income	19%	20%
8th-Gr. Math not low-income	46%	46%
Source: NAEP		

Proficiency levels have been declining since 2003 in Kansas, while Florida is showing solid gains, and that has parents and legislators asking a lot of questions. But instead of taking corrective action, Porter and other education officials try to dupe citizens.

Randy Watson, the state commissioner of schools, and Brad Neuenswander, deputy commissioner, participated in the hearing, but they did not attempt to correct Porter's statements.

A pattern of deception

Jim Porter was first elected to the Kansas State Board of Education in 2015.[53] His biography says he worked in public education for forty-seven years before retiring, including thirty-four years as a superintendent.

He should be well-versed in student achievement and school finance with his background. Still, he has a habit of making inaccurate and misleading statements.

Porter made many deceptive statements in a 2016 guest column published in many Kansas newspapers. He said an accounting change related to state support for special education made it appear that total funding had increased, saying, "Until recently, special education funds were sent directly to the Cooperative or Interlocal. However, a few years ago, those funds were sent to the local public school, and the school then sent those funds to the provider of services. This was lauded as an increase in public school funding when, in fact, it was the same amount but just laundered through the public schools."[54]

But according to an email from Deputy Commissioner of Finance Dale Dennis, special education funding had been provided directly to school districts "for at least ten years."[55] Mr. Porter didn't define "recently," but most people would take it to mean within the time frame he referenced (since 2011), and that is not the case. Also, special education co-ops are not separate entities. A school district hosts them, so money would not have been sent directly to co-ops as Porter claimed but to the host school district.

Porter also said an accounting change related to funding for pensions artificially increased school funding, saying, "Until recently, the state contribution to the Kansas Public Employees Retirement

System [KPERS] was sent directly to KPERS. Now the funds are transferred to the public school account and then transferred to KPERS on the same day. Again, this was lauded as an increase to public school funding even though it was the same amount of money with just an additional transfer from the State of Kansas to the school to KEPRS."

Another email from Dale Dennis said KPERS funding has been sent directly to school districts and included in the reported funding totals since 2005.[56] Again, Porter doesn't define "recently," but most people would take it to mean within the time frame he references (since 2011), which was not valid.

He also tried to pull a fast one in discussing school districts' cash reserves: "[F]or the past several years, many schools are having to use fund balances to meet current needs. Those schools that do not have fund balances have to make cuts in services to kids to survive. Spending fund balances is like an individual using their savings account on their monthly expenses."

The criticism wasn't about having fund balances; every entity needs some degree of reserves. The complaint was that many school districts were building cash reserves because administrators weren't spending all of the tax money provided to educate students.

Figure 6 shows school districts collectively had $468.1 million in operating cash reserves on July 1, 2005. By 2015 (the last update before Porter's column), the total had ballooned to $853 million. Most of the $385 million increase represented funding from prior years that was not used to educate students.

Additional examples of education officials deceiving the legislature are documented later in this book.

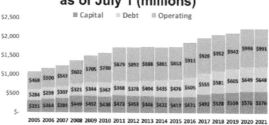

Fig. 6: Operating Cash Reserves as of July 1 (millions)

Deception in the courtroom

Statements made in committee hearings of the Kansas Legislature are not sworn testimony because conferees are not testifying under oath. But education officials have made deceptive statements even in court.

Since the turn of the century, the public school system and the legislature have been in litigation over school funding more often than not. The current case, *Gannon v. Kansas*, was filed in November 2010. The court issued a final ruling in 2019, but it still has jurisdiction at the time of publication.[57]

The Kansas Supreme Court effectively ordered the legislature to increase funding by about $1.1 billion after determining that schools were not adequately funded. (The court ignored legal precedent and overlooked or misapplied facts in the record to reach its opinion, but that is another story briefly addressed later in this book).

The testimony of a school superintendent about changes related to a federal grant for an elementary school served as the poster child for the court's cavalier approach to analyzing the issue of adequacy, and deception exists throughout that testimony. Mike O'Neal, an attorney and former Speaker of the Kansas House of Representatives, describes the situation:

The Supreme Court cited Emerson, in USD 500 in Kansas City, Kansas, for the proposition that more money (federal) made a significant difference in student achievement there. The Court opined:

"Illustrative of the substantial competent evidence supporting the panel's finding of a correlation between funding and student achievement in the state is Emerson Elementary School of Kansas City, with a demographic breakdown of approximately 50% African American and 48% Hispanic students. Dr. Cynthia Lane, the district's superintendent, testified that in 2009 Emerson had been declared the worst performing elementary school in Kansas. But new funding through federal grants led to implementation of programs and policy changes that helped dramatically increase student achievement. After 3 years, students moved from Math and ELA state proficiency rates of 30% to 85%."

After acknowledging that the State had presented evidence and argument of contrary views about the Emerson Elementary experience, the Court rejected that evidence and sided with the lower court panel, presumably because it fit the simple narrative the Court was most enamored with—that more money means better outcomes. The court was mistaken to so quickly dismiss the rest of this Emerson story. So, what evidence was there in the record to show the fatally flawed Emerson Elementary analysis? A look at the District Superintendent's own sworn testimony is telling.

At trial, testimony was elicited from the District's Superintendent as quoted above in the *Gannon* Supreme Court decision. What the Court failed to note was the balance of her testimony regarding how she claimed the performance turnaround occurred.[58]

Lane testified that the roughly $3 million federal grant "had everything to do with the turnaround because without that, we wouldn't have been able to purchase the—we have a lot of technology now the children are using and are learning."

That may be her opinion, but the facts tell a different story.

Lane testified that meetings with the Emerson staff revealed about 50% of them did not believe that the children could learn at high levels of expectations. So they replaced the principal and roughly half the staff before launching the federal grant program. Pairing children with teachers who believed in them unquestionably makes a difference, but Lane discounted that and gave money all the credit.

The district also could have purchased the technology without a federal grant. USD 500 Kansas City area had $25.5 million in operating cash reserves in 2005; the total increased to $50.2 million at the beginning of the grant period. Most of the increase is tax money received to educate students but not spent. Lane had multiple options to purchase technology without a federal grant, but that didn't fit her narrative.

She also neglected to share information with the court that refuted her claim that spending money is required for better student achievement.

David Dorsey, a former school teacher and senior education policy fellow with Kansas Policy Institute, tells the rest of the story:

The same year Emerson Elementary was awarded its SIG [school improvement grant], another USD 500 school, Northwest Middle School, was awarded a similar grant with a higher amount of $4.77 million. Northwest has similar minority and economically disadvantaged populations to Emerson Elementary (just over half African American and just over one-third Hispanic and 98% low income). But the outcomes pursuant to the SIG were very much dissimilar, indeed.[59]

Northwest Middle School had an uptick in results the first year, but declines over the next two years resulted in a net decrease over the grant period. Lane didn't tell the court that Northwest received more money than Emerson but saw results fall.

Lane also gave testimony contradictory to her statement in a district newsletter dated March 12, 2012.[60]

The U.S. Department of Education denied a portion of the district's proposal to raise standards in a requested waiver from the Kansas Approved Accountability Plan from USDOE. Lane responded, saying, "The Kansas assessment is not rigorous enough to guarantee that our students are on-track with where they need to be. We have asked to raise standards for our students by administering the MAP, which is a more rigorous assessment, and USDOE is telling us 'No!'"

The employee newsletter in which this quote appears makes no mention of funding; she blames academic issues solely on sub-standard assessment issues.

Lane didn't confine her deception to legal testimony. For example, a 2015 story in the *Kansas City Star*[61] outlining the district's plans to reduce spending contained multiple financial misrepresentations. One of Lane's deceptions was a claim that her district was losing $2 million in state aid, but Department of Education records reflected a $12.8 million *increase*.[62]

Superintendent deceives parent, won't substantiate claims
To hear Topeka Superintendent Tiffany Anderson talk about student achievement in her district, you would think it is pretty good overall. But as is often the case with education officials, the facts tell a shockingly different story.

Anderson's email response to a parent's inquiry said "various schools" made academic gains. She said, "[T]he majority of our schools have steadily improved." And while acknowledging that "continued progress is needed," Anderson noted that "in 2019, 23 of the 26 TPS schools increased in math or English on state tests and in 2019 and 2021, numerous schools outperformed the state on the state standardized assessments."[63]

Nowhere does Anderson cite specific results, and that is because the facts are pretty ugly:

- 64% of high school students are below grade level in math, and only 10% are on track for college and career.
- 48% of high school students are below grade level in English language arts, and just 17% are on track.
- For all students tested in grades three through eight and ten, 48% are below grade level in math, and only 17% are proficient; in English language arts, the results are 44% and 23%, respectively.

Anderson was asked to provide documentation to substantiate her statements, but she did not respond. The director of instruction for the district merely sent links to the state website. But even without her documentation, one can examine each school's overall performance over time.

Kansas Policy Institute's A–F Grading System translates state assessment scores into letter grades based on the KSDE cut scores and definitions.[64] A letter grade, like a student report card, is assigned to each public and private school taking the state assessment based on a formula, with equal weighting applied to individual letter grades to calculate a grade point average. Each grade level tested by KSDE (grades three to eight and ten) is assigned a grade for English language arts and math for low-income kids and those who aren't low-income; so each grade tested earns four letter grades.

On this basis, eighteen schools showed improvement from 2018 to 2019; seven schools declined, and two had the same GPA. But only two of the seventeen did better than in 2017. Two were the same as in 2017, one wasn't open in 2017, and the other thirteen partially recovered from declines in 2018 but were still below their 2017 GPA. Anderson didn't mention this important information.

No schools in the district received an "A" in 2019, and only one—McClure Elementary—got a "B." There were twelve with a "C," eleven with a "D," and three received an "F." Topeka's grades were even worse in 2021; five schools with a "C," thirteen with a "D," and nine with an "F."[65] (And yes, there are twenty-seven schools, not twenty-six as Anderson stated.)

As for Anderson's comparing Topeka to state averages, some Topeka schools have higher scores than state averages for each subject/grade/cohort, but that isn't a high bar. It's akin to having a "C-" with the state average at a "D+." Most scores for Topeka schools are below state averages.

Anderson's email is typical of the statewide efforts to keep the truth of student achievement from parents—relatively meaningless word salads and some arguably false claims. For example, the data does not show that most Topeka schools "have steadily improved in performance."

In another example, she says, "[T]he schools with challenges are being closely monitored and they are using resources to address academic progress." State law requires districts to conduct annual needs assessments of each school to identify learning barriers and make the appropriate budgetary adjustments. But an audit of twenty-five of the largest school districts last year revealed that Topeka is one of many districts that could not produce any record of having done so.[66] This issue is explored in greater detail in Chapter 4.

Parents should be able to trust education officials to be straight with them, but in most cases, they cannot.

*State and local school board members won't say how long it will take
to get all students to grade level*

Education officials and their attorneys told courts that lack of money
was holding students back, and the courts bought the excuse. In
Gannon IV, issued in March 2017, the state supreme court said that
having a quarter of students tested below grade level, which the
court used as a proxy for achieving the minimum standards, somehow proved that schools were underfunded.[67]

No research exists proving that simply spending more money
causes student achievement to improve, of course, but school
officials made that claim, and now they don't want to be held accountable for their beliefs.

Funding continues to increase, but as discussed in Chapter 1,
about a third of students are below grade level; about a quarter
were below grade level in 2016, and the decline cannot be blamed
on the pandemic. Kansas Policy Institute asked eleven school superintendents how long they thought it would take to get all students
to at least grade level. Not one would speculate a guess. Their
silence—likely because the honest answer is "never"—speaks volumes about the likelihood of those kids being successful in life
without intervention from the state legislature.[68]

Dodge City Deputy Superintendent Dr. Scott Springston didn't
answer the question, but he sent a lengthy respectful response to
what he said was a fair question: "While this response has not provided a direct response to the question posed, it is a fair response as
educating students is way too complex. USD 443's goal is to have
all students at grade level in literacy and Math as measured by the
[state assessment test]."[69]

Springston is measuring achievement against the state assessment, but Hutchinson Superintendent Michael Folks claimed the
performance on the state assessment is not the target: "In regard
to the question regarding the state assessment tables you provided
and the court's targets: the data is old information and is not in a
format provided by KSDE. Assuming you put these charts together?
I would state you're not using language provided in the past by
KSDE and these are your perceptions and verbiage on the old data.

We are focusing on multiple measures and data points instead of using the Kansas state assessments as our indicators of growth . . . ."[70]

But in reality, the data was the most recent available from the Kansas Department of Education. It isn't in a format provided by KSDE because local districts and KSDE won't present their data so that parents understand reality, but it is their data.

Wichita Superintendent Alicia Thompson also declined to estimate how long it would take the district to get all students to grade level. But she did qualify student achievement as "not good enough."

Andover, Blue Valley, Shawnee Mission, Gardner-Edgerton, Olathe, Spring Hill, De Soto, and Kansas City superintendents would not respond.

Ask superintendents about their devotion to diversity and equity, and they will talk your ear off. But their unwillingness to even estimate how long it will take them to get all students to grade-level is another indication that many students won't have a chance to be successful in life without legislative intervention.

State school board members also declined to answer the question. During the public comment portion of the November 9, 2021, state school board meeting, board members were asked to respond to these two questions:

1. How many years—or decades—will it take Kansas to get kids to grade level?
2. Have you changed the official achievement standards that you approved in 2015?[71]

None of the ten board members would respond to either question.

These examples in Chapter 2 demonstrate a pattern of deception over Kansas's sad state of student achievement from state and local education officials. That pattern extends back many years, and the deceit has intensified as parents become more aware of the facts.

The education bureaucracy puts its spin on an old maxim—"If you can't win the game, change the rules." State and local officials refuse to accept responsibility for resolving race-based and income-based educational discrimination, so they are de-emphasizing achievement and measuring success by other means.

Chapter 3—How the System De-emphasizes Achievement and Redefines Success

Eddie Haskell was a character on the 1950s television show *Leave It to Beaver*. Haskell was a duplicitous and conniving teenager, except when speaking to adults. Then he was the embodiment of virtue and politeness.

The Kansas public school bureaucracy bears a lot of resemblance to Eddie Haskell. Legislators and parents hear things like, "It's all about the kids" and "Achievement is our number one priority." But the bureaucracy's actions tell a different story.

One high-profile instance was on display at the December 1, 2021, Special Committee on Education hearing. State school board member Ann Mah testified in response to the question, "Is the application of Critical Race Theory or any derivative thereof finding its way into classrooms?"

> The board simply says that CRT—Critical Race Theory—is an advanced and complex framework of analysis that goes back to the '70s that examines how racism is inherent in our legal institutions. It's largely studied in law school. You won't find it anywhere in our state standards, and you will not find it anywhere in our assessments, so it's a little difficult to say that CRT is influencing student achievement.
>
> The problem that we have is that the term "CRT" has been co-opted to be an umbrella term for anything anybody has to complain about in public schools.[72]

Mah and the other education officials condescendingly tell parents and legislators that their eyes are lying to them—just like the weavers said to the emperor and his followers.

Mah's claim is a conscious deception shrouded in semantics. There may be no tenets of critical race theory in state standards or state assessments as something to be taught, but she knows that that is entirely separate from classroom activity.

Examples abound across Kansas, like the teacher training material in the Blue Valley school district that says, "People who are white, male, heterosexual, upper-middle-class, athletic, able-bodied, or neurotypical are in the Dominant Culture. People who do not fall under one of those identities are part of the subordinate culture."[73]

The Shawnee Mission school district spent $400,000 on Deep Equity training, which Jeffrey Arant said was a factor in resigning his teaching position.

"Deep Equity being taught in our school district was the deciding factor [in leaving the district]," Arant said. "If we sent our children to our school district where Deep Equity is being taught, they would be singled out because of a characteristic they had no choice in—race . . . I'm not sure how my soon-to-be kindergartener can have a healthy and meaningful friendship with another child when they see him as an oppressor."[74]

Arant says Deep Equity training is mandatory and is done "under the guise of professional development during in-service days."[75]

CRT indoctrination also exists in small rural districts. Four days after Superintendent Lonnie Moser sent a letter to parents stating unequivocally that "Critical Race Theory" is not being taught in the Hiawatha, Kansas, district, former teacher Stuart Aller told the school board that CRT is part of the district's culture.[76]

Aller said the tenets of critical race theory exist under the guise of the district's Diversity and Inclusion Council: "I'm concerned that this council . . . is an indoctrination and discrimination tool," Aller said. "We received staff and student training that places blame for societal problems on those having white skin color."[77]

After Ann Mah testified that CRT isn't in classrooms, a parade of parents cited examples of their children being indoctrinated with its tenets.

Senator Molly Baumgardner also cited an email she received the night before from a parent. The parent shared,

My child is biracial. And based on what is being said in the school by the teacher, [my child] needs to decide "is one parent bad and one parent good because of skin color?" And that is being presented as fact in the classroom. Not discussion, not let's research, not let's look at things, but presented as fact. To hear from a parent of a grade school child, being told, "the assignment for today is write a sentence that explains why you're sorry for being white."

I don't want to hear that those kinds of things are happening in our schools. And we can say, "That's not CRT," but it sure as heck is not educational equity. But those are the kinds of things that are happening in our school, and we can come up with a new name for it, but those are the things that parents are hearing from their children when they come home. And that's creating a whole new dimension of what I would refer to as mental health stressors. And a whole dimension as to why parents are losing faith in what is occurring in our schools.

I learned long ago that the number one concern of a parent . . . of their child going to school is, "Is my child safe?" Second concern, "Will my child learn?" And what we're hearing from parents is, from an emotional standpoint, they don't necessarily think their kids are safe when these things are being taught or lectured in a classroom. So those are the areas, we can take CRT, we can take DEI [diversity, equity, and inclusion], move all of those titles or identifiers out of the way, but the bottom line is, we know these things are happening in the classroom.

Mah offered nothing in rebuttal but disagreed that parents had lost confidence in schools. Her blithe dismissal of Baumgardner's concerns prompted Senator Renee Erickson to speak:

As I sit here and listen to the dialogue, and I've sat here for the last day and a half listening to the dialogue, this probably exemplifies the most frustrating thing about being a public education teacher or principal, which I was proudly for twenty years.

We lose sight of the kids. If it weren't for, and I've said this many times, if it weren't for our teachers and our building staff and our school secretaries who wear fifty million hats, if it weren't for those people, because of those people what we're seeing here today, thank God we have dedicated teachers and building staff members because that is the only thing keeping this system afloat. So let me be abundantly clear about that.

But when things happen like what are happening here today, it doesn't hurt me; quite frankly, it doesn't hurt you, Board Member Mah. It hurts our kids. Because the problems that we have are adult-manufactured problems, and that's what we're seeing today. And shame on us for that being the case because our kids are paying the price.

Erickson then spoke of a meeting between legislators and state school board members:

I was not privy to a meeting where legislators were invited to the state board recently, but I did watch following the state board meetings. I had not talked to any legislators about that, but I did after I watched the state board meetings. There were accusations by state board members that legislators had a list of lies and that they came in threatening state board members. And when that happens after the fact in a public setting, we need to be able to clear the air and focus on the facts. We have the facts of what's happening in our schools. And after all this time, we should have some solutions. And we have the funding. So, I would like to see us put aside adult issues and work together for the children. They deserve it. We owe it to them. And we need to put aside our adult issues and be honest and get the solutions our kids need because right now they are not succeeding at any level that should be acceptable to anyone in this room.

Mah responded with less credibility and sincerity than Eddie Haskell:

We have worked successfully together, and we would like to continue that. In fact, we suggested that during the legislative session, we have a caucus between the legislature and the state board ongoing throughout the session. Because as you said, and I agree, it happens on both sides. These adult things like CRT is an adult-made-up thing. It's a high-level, graduate-level course. We don't teach it.

Saying positive things with zero sincerity is a long-established pattern of the education bureaucracy. It's like someone saying, "Well, bless your heart," instead of "Screw you."

Mah gave another example of their disingenuity at that same hearing: "Academics is our first concern. Student achievement is our number one goal. And that's why it's our number one foundational structure in KESA [Kansas Education Systems Accreditation]."

The department of education says a successful Kansas high school graduate has the academic preparation, cognitive preparation, technical skills, employability skills, and civic engagement to be successful in post-secondary education, in the attainment of an industry-recognized certification, or in the workforce, without the need for remediation.[78]

That may sound like academic preparation is the "number one goal" (as intended), but then the state board's Outcomes for Measuring Progress show it to be merely window dressing. The department of education website lists "academically prepared for post-secondary" in the Quantitative Measures section, but it is not used in public presentations.[79]

Fig. 7: Outcomes for Measuring Progress

- Social/emotional growth measured locally
- Kindergarten readiness
- Individual Plan of Study focused on career interest
- High school graduation rates
- Postsecondary completion/attendance

The Outcomes for Measuring Progress in Figure 7 appear in information packets for state board of education meetings and public presentations.[80]

If listing order indicates the state board's priorities, social/emotional growth measurement must be the top concern. State board members have responsibility for the K–12 system, not pre-schools, yet kindergarten readiness is their second measurement. The third is having an individualized plan of study for every student, but the target is whether one exists on paper, not its effectiveness.

High school graduation rates, as discussed earlier, may reflect attendance but not students' achievement. The final measure of progress—post-secondary complete/attendance—mostly tracks activity rather than learning. The post-secondary success rate is the percentage of high school graduates who either earned an industry-recognized certification or a higher education degree or *continued their education two years after graduation* (emphasis added).[81]

After two years of working toward an industry certification or a college degree, students still in school are counted as successful (the "attendance" piece of the success measurement). Like high school graduation rates, this measurement ignores effectiveness.

The PowerPoint presentation used at the fifty-city Success Tour referenced previously showed changes in graduation rates and post-secondary completion/ attendance, but not academic preparedness.[82] The public would not see progress, let alone success, had they done so.

The state website says, "For Kansas to achieve its vision for education in the area of academic preparation, 75% of all students need to score at or above Levels 3 and 4 on state assessments."[83] As shown earlier in Tables 4 and 5, only 28% of students were in those levels in math, and just 35% in English language arts. Those results are worse than when the department's Vision for Education was established in 2016, and the declines existed pre-COVID.

The department of education and the state board of education give the appearance that achievement is their top priority, but evidence of achievement being honestly discussed and measured is hard to find.

Sadly for students and parents, the department of education and the state board of education several years ago placed a higher priority on things other than what most parents believe should be the top priority—academically preparing students for college and career.

Creating the illusion of improvement
Jim Steinmeyer, a designer of magic illusions, said, "The art of a magician is not found in the simple deception, but in what surrounds it, the construction of a reality which supports the illusion."[84]

President Bill Clinton signed Improving America's Schools Act (IASA) in 1994. Its main components were:

Title I—Helping Disadvantaged Children Meet High Standards
Title II—Dwight D. Eisenhower Professional Development Program
Title III—Technology for Education
Title IV—Safe and Drug-Free Schools
Title V—Promoting Equity
Title VI—Innovative Education Program Strategies
Title VII—Bi-Lingual Education, Language Enhancement, and
    Language Acquisition Programs
Title VIII—Impact Aid
Title IX—Indian, Native Hawaiian, and Alaska Native Education
Title X—Programs of National Significance
Title XI—Coordinated Services
Title XII—School Facilities
Title XIII—Support and Assistance Programs to Improve Education
Title XIV—General Provisions[85]

IASA was part of the Clinton administration's education re-form efforts, and it re-authorized the Elementary and Secondary Education Act (ESEA) of 1965. Clinton signed IASA at a school in Framingham, Massachusetts, surrounded by Senators Ted Kennedy and Ed Markey, a gymnasium full of cheering students, and other dignitaries.[86]

Clinton told the students,

This bill is about you. It's not about all of us politicians up here, it's about you. It's about your future. The age in which you are growing up and the world toward which you are going can be the best time America ever had. It will be exciting, and our diversity in America is a gold mine of opportunity. No other country is so well-positioned to move into the twenty-first century, to live in a global society that is more peaceful and more secure. No one.

But it all depends upon whether we develop the God-given capacity of every boy and girl in this country no matter where they live, no matter what their racial or ethnic or religious background is. That's your challenge. Let's do it together.

Table 11 shows that 30% of fourth-grade students in the United States were considered proficient in reading on the 1994 National Assessment of Educational Progress. But six years later, only 29% were proficient. In politics, that means it is time for a new scheme.

Table 11: 4th-Grade Reading Proficiency			
Year	Below Basic	Basic	Proficient+
1994	40%	31%	30%
2000	41%	30%	29%
2009	33%	34%	33%
2019	34%	31%	35%
Source: NAEP, all students			

President George W. Bush signed No Child Left Behind in 2001 as another update to ESEA. The goal of NCLB was to have 100% of public school students proficient by 2014.[87] Of course, everyone knew that was impossible, so Congress helped state education departments create the illusion of proficiency by letting each state develop its own definitions.

As documented in "Removing Barriers to Better Public Education," the Kansas Department of Education and the State Board of Education took advantage of the opportunity to redefine proficiency by creating new standards in 2002. It was an illusion that would make David Copperfield proud.

The 2002 standards replaced those that had been in effect since 2000. The performance categories in 2000 and 2001 were Advanced, Proficient, Satisfactory, Basic, and Unsatisfactory. Table 12 shows department officials changed the performance categories in 2002 to Exemplary, Advanced, Proficient, Basic, and Unsatisfactory. Proficient went from being the second-highest category to the third-highest category.[88]

Table 12: State Assessment Performance Categories Listed in Descending Order of Achievement		
2000	2002	2006
Advanced	Exemplary	Exemplary
Proficient	Advanced	Advanced
Satisfactory	Proficient	Proficient
Basic	Basic	Approaches Standard
Unsatisfactory	Unsatisfactory	Academic Warning
Source: Kansas Dept. of Education		

Department officials confirm that the same assessment was given in 2000 and 2002; they also acknowledge that the five levels of cut scores remained intact.[89] So the only thing that changed was the labels. "Advanced" was changed to "Exemplary," "Proficient" was renamed "Advanced," and what was previously considered "Satisfactory" was suddenly "Proficient."

The percentage of correct answers required for each performance category, which was already deceptively low, became an absolute farce.

As shown in Table 13, a student needed just 60% of correct answers in math in 2000 and 2001 to be Proficient (the second-highest performance level), but from 2002 through 2005, they only needed 48% of correct answers to be Proficient.

A student getting 48% on a regular math test would be an "F," but when the bureaucracy evaluates itself, 48% is Proficient.

Table 13: Minimum % Correct Required for Each Performance Category			
Reading Assessments			
2000 and 2001		2002 through 2005	
Performance Level	Minimun Correct	Performance Level	Minimun Correct
Advanced	93%	Exemplary	93%
Proficient	87%	Advanced	87%
Satisfactory	80%	Proficient	80%
Basic	68%	Basic	68%
Unsatisfactory	<68%	Unsatisfactory	<68%
Math Assessments			
2000 and 2001		2002 through 2005	
Performance Level	Minimun Correct	Performance Level	Minimun Correct
Advanced	75%	Exemplary	75%
Proficient	60%	Advanced	60%
Satisfactory	48%	Proficient	48%
Basic	35%	Basic	35%
Unsatisfactory	<35%	Unsatisfactory	<35%
Source: Kansas Dept. of Education			

The impact of reducing standards in this manner is quite evident. Simply by changing the labels, the percentage of students considered to be Proficient in 2001 went from the low 30s in most grade levels to the low 60s in 2002.

Of course, that deception was not shared with the public because that would have given away the illusion.

It is also noteworthy that the department of education did not contest any of these findings. Education officials were given a copy of the report in advance of publication to provide them with a chance to correct anything inaccurate. They chose not to respond.[90]

"Kansans Can" initiative de-emphasizes academic preparation

There was a time when many experts thought school choice would never come to Kansas, mainly because parents had a false impression of high achievement. But a multi-year public awareness effort helped legislators understand that outcomes fell far short of the hype, particularly for low-income students.

Finally, the legislature approved the state's first school choice program in 2014. The Tax Credit for Low-Income Students Scholarship Act provides a 70% state income tax credit for contributions made to a non-profit scholarship-granting organization (SGO). The SGO uses the donations to grant scholarships up to $8,000 for qualifying students. Over one thousand students attended eighty private schools during the 2022 school year (despite annual efforts by the education lobby to shut the program down).[91]

Department of education officials and state school board members loudly complained about the content of the public awareness effort, but they could not say that the content was inaccurate.

In 2015, they launched a series of listening tours around the state under the new commissioner of education, Dr. Randy Watson. Participants were asked what they wanted from the public school system, what they thought might be missing, what skills graduates should possess, etc. But participants had no clue that a quarter of students were below grade level, and only a third were proficient. So it's not surprising that academics were much less frequently identified as a "lacking" skill.

Watson and other officials seized on this to say, "It's time to redesign schools!"[92]

They gave it a catchy moniker of "Kansans Can" with the unbelievable vision that "Kansas leads the world in the success of each student." There is a meaningless nod to "demanding higher standards in academic skills." But the real goal is de-emphasizing academic preparation in favor of "employability and citizenship skills."[93]

David Dorsey described it as rearranging deck chairs on a sinking ship in the name of reform.[94]

He puts an experienced educator's perspective on Kansans Can's five "new directions":

- **Kindergarten readiness:** This is education code for universal pre-K, which sounds like a great idea. Unfortunately, it isn't. Recent research from across the political spectrum, from the Brookings Institute to the Heritage Foundation, shows that universal pre-K has no long-term impacts on student learning. Oh sure, kids may learn sooner the difference between green and blue, a two and a three, or a cow and a horse. They may even be better prepared for kindergarten (remember when kindergarten was there to prepare for first grade?), but evidence points to those in pre-K losing whatever gains they had by third grade.
- **Individual Plan of Study Focused on Career Interest:** Conceptually, this has great potential. It would seem a good thing that students get focused on a post-secondary and/ or career interest as they are getting close to finishing high school. However, this is another one of those "devil in the details" ideas. Who is going to administer such an undertaking? Imagine a thousand-student high school in which someone or some several will have to develop, maintain, and update those plans. Could that really happen? Those of us who have been involved directly in the special education process know how difficult it is to keep up with an IEP (Individual Education Plan). Think of this individual plan as an IEP for every student.
- **High school graduation rates:** Kansans Can says, "We need to make sure every student graduates with the skills needed to be successful as they enter college or the workforce." Kinda sounds like a take on No Child Left Behind (NCLB). Sure, a 100% graduation rate is a noble goal, but

seriously, do you think it is incumbent on the schools to make sure everyone graduates? It wasn't long ago that we were rolling our collective eyes at the prospect of making sure "no child is left behind." Now those who were critical of NCLB have come up with their own 100%, no exceptions version—ironic, to be sure. KSDE says the graduation rate is already 85.7%, but we know from ACT scores and anecdotes from employers that most of those who graduate aren't ready for the next step in life. How about making sure that a diploma means something? Maybe it's time Kansas does as some other states do and offer differentiated diplomas. Indiana is a good example. They offer three different diploma programs: a basic, one with academic honors, and one with technical honors. Students who are going on to post-secondary education might be better prepared and enjoy more success if they earn a more stringent high school diploma that reflects a course of study aligned with future plans.

- **Post-secondary Completion/Attendance:** This is another admirable goal, but it also underscores a fundamental problem with the education system, from kindergarten through post-secondary. K–12 education is still organizationally separate from post-secondary education. If more students are going to be successful educationally beyond high school, there needs to be better coordination with those in post-secondary education. There has to be a seamless transition from one to another, but unfortunately that is not the case. How does K–12 address the issue of higher education getting more and more expensive, leaving students with the prospect of taking on more and more debt as they leave higher education? Couple that with the fact that those leaving college have a more difficult time finding employment after graduation; how could K–12 on their own possibly change that?

- **Social/Emotional Growth Measured Locally:** Who could argue with the importance of having social and emotional skills? But what is confusing is that Kansans Can wants these skills to be "measured locally." What does that mean? Does it mean the state thinks they are very important but again doesn't want to tell school districts that they must teach them? Is it just window dressing, meaning Kansans Can recognizes the importance of those factors, but they have no way to teach them (curriculum)? But those questions aside, it brings up yet another, one that is more fundamental to the role of the education system: is it appropriate for schools to be spending precious time taking on another set of skills to be taught when the schools struggle with the academic curriculum? And furthermore, aren't many of those skills developed within the household? Of course, those are important skills to have, but how much of the entire "student package" is the responsibility of the school? Is the school system really going to teach empathy and other emotional "skills"? Where does it stop? At what opportunity cost? How are the local districts to measure those skills? A different set of assessments? All those questions should be explored before being thrust upon a system that doesn't do a very good job of performing the tasks currently at hand.

The hype goes beyond "leads the world in the success of every student." They made the initial phase of the school redesign aspect of Kansans Can analogous to the NASA Mercury phase of sending a man to the moon. Subsequent groups of school districts joining the voluntary redesign project are Gemini I, Gemini II, Apollo I, Apollo II, and Apollo III.

Watson announced the first seven school districts selected for the redesign project at the August 2017 state school board meeting.

Dorsey unpacks the hype of the Mercury 7 promotional venture.[95]

"Why seven? Because Commissioner Watson is making the redesign project analogous to the Mercury phase of sending a man to the moon. Project Mercury had the seven original astronauts, and the state board selected seven of the 29 school districts that applied. Each has been paired with one of those astronauts. Coffeyville (district) is John Glenn, Liberal (district) is Alan Shepard; you get the idea."

Fig. 8: School Redesign Project

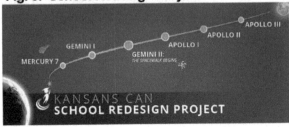

The Mercury 7 districts had to redesign one elementary and one middle/high school around the five spokes of the Kansans Can wheel: kindergarten readiness, individual plans of study, graduation rates, post-secondary completion/attendance, and social/emotional growth. There was no additional funding and no waivers of state laws involved. Commissioner Watson said, "We're doing all of this with existing resources, no new buildings, and the same educators."[96]

Table 14 shows that the Mercury 7 redesign experiment has been a dismal academic failure.

Table 14: Mercury 7 Districts - Math Proficiency			
School District	2017	2019	2021
Coffeyville	24%	16%	12%
Liberal	16%	12%	7%
McPherson	26%	28%	25%
Olathe	43%	42%	37%
Stockton	18%	13%	11%
Twin Valley	38%	32%	33%
Wellington	34%	21%	21%
Source: Kansas Dept. of Education; all students tested			

Each district has lower math proficiency (Levels 3 and 4, on track for college and career). Coffeyville dropped from 24% proficient in 2017 to 12% in 2021. Proficiency plummeted from 16% to 7% in Liberal, 18% to 11% in Stockton, and 34% to 21% in Wellington. Olathe and Twin Valley experienced less-pronounced drops, 43% to 37% and 38% to 33%, respectively.

Attempts to blame the declines on COVID don't hold up to scrutiny, as all but one district—McPherson—had pre-COVID proficiency reductions.

As of March 2022, only 71 of the state's 286 school districts participated in the redesign project.[97]

Accreditation emphasizes process over academics
Adherence to Kansans Can is the basis for school district accreditation in the Kansas Education Systems Accreditation (KESA).[98]

Full implementation of KESA began during the 2017–18 school year. Previously, accreditation was granted at the individual building level and, according to the department of education, focused on a set of assurances rather than a systemwide or district process.[99]

The switch to accrediting districts instead of buildings indicates that academics are being de-emphasized. A poorly performing building could lose accreditation in the past, but its performance is masked in a district-wide accreditation system.

The accreditation criteria are KESA compliance, KESA Foundational Structures, KESA Goal Areas & Statements, Procedures and Policies for Long-term Sustainability, Results—State Board Goals, and KESA Process.[100] Accreditation is almost entirely about process and compliance, with only one criterion mentioning academic outcomes.

KESA Goal Areas & Statements requires districts to show "evidence, supported by data (quantitative and qualitative), of results in all goal statements." But school districts get to set their own goals (minimum of two), with the caveat that they must be measurable, challenging, and will result in "an impact on student learning."

The Results: State Board Goals criterion is not about improving academic preparation for college and career but about the five State Board Goal areas of kindergarten readiness, social-emotional factors, individual plans of study, graduation rate, and post-secondary success.

A comparison of accreditation reports presented to the state board of education at its January 2021 meeting demonstrates the focus on process over academics.[101]

The Coffeyville School District passed all but one of the accreditation criteria. The Accreditation Review Council initially gave the Coffeyville conditional accreditation but approved full accreditation upon appeal. The ARC decided that the district's Strategic Plan provided the information missing from the initial evaluation.

St. Paul Elementary in the Kansas City Diocese passed every accreditation criteria but was given conditional accreditation because there was "no evidence of an IPS (Individual Plan of Study)" for eighth graders. The ARC also said it was not evident that data was used in decision-making. St. Paul's disputed the findings, but their appeal was denied.

Table 15: Math Assessment Performance in 2019			
School District	Below Grade Level	At Grade Level, Needs Remedial Training	On Track for College & Career
St. Paul Elementary	22%	43%	35%
Coffeyville Elementary	39%	44%	18%
Coffeyville district	41%	42%	16%
Source:KSDE; may not equal 100% due to rounding			

Table 15 shows student achievement seems to be of no consequence to the accreditation policy in Kansas. St. Paul's may not have an individual plan of study for eighth graders, but they have superior performance on the state assessment. Students are twice as likely to be proficient in math as the elementary school in Coffeyville (35% vs. 18%). Coffeyville elementary students are about twice as likely to be below grade level. (Table 15 references 2019 state assessment results because they were the most current during the accreditation process.)

Only 16% of all the students in the Coffeyville School District are proficient, but they get fully accredited because they have the requisite processes in place. Those processes are ineffective at producing proficiency, but process rules over academics at the Kansas State Department of Education.

Bonuses for DEI, but not for academic improvement
Berkshire Hathaway vice chairman Charlie Munger's quote about incentives—"Show me the incentive, and I will show you the outcome"—puts perspective on dismal student achievement in Kansas.[102]

There are no incentives to improve (or consequences for *not* improving), but some local school boards incentivize other behavior.

USD 233 Olathe Superintendent Dr. Brent Yeager can earn a $25,000 annual bonus for implementing the school board's diversity and other objectives, but not for improving the district's weak academic performance.[103]

Yeager's five evaluation objectives for the 2021–22 school year are:

- Navigate the pandemic (30%)
- Relaunch the Strategic Plan (20%)
- Diversity and Engagement (20%)
- Communications (15%)
- Successful establishment of the District's next bond referendum (15%)

There is only an amorphous reference to academic performance in its five-year Strategic Plan, rewritten last fall due to COVID-19 considerations: a guaranteed and viable curriculum to ensure that all students are on or above grade level.

But that is only about having a curriculum in place that, in the superintendent's opinion, can "ensure" that students are at least at grade level. The Strategic Plan doesn't identify current achievement levels, let alone a timeline for getting kids to grade level.[104]

According to the department of education's 2021 state assessment, nearly a quarter of all Olathe students are below grade level in math and English language arts, and the numbers are worse for high school students (38% below grade level in math, 25% below grade level in ELA). Even worse, achievement was declining before the pandemic, and that sad truth is also missing from the Strategic Plan.

Four of Yeager's five objectives identify specific goals, but those are more about pushing a narrative than anything else. For example, the Communications objective list includes:

- "Tell our story on social media (short, sweet communications that describes [*sic*] who we are as a district ex: # of languages spoken, number of schools, number of chicken nuggets served each year."
- "Establish communication processes to support the board of education (talking points, district email, and boilerplate responses)."

One goal under Relaunching the Strategic Plan is to define measurable objectives for a public scorecard. The district posted an Academic Scorecard, but it is horribly inaccurate.[105] It says third-grade reading proficiency is 69% and fourth-grade math proficiency is 84%. According to KSDE's January 2018 application to the U.S. Department of Education for approval of the state plan to comply with the Elementary and Secondary Education Act, "Levels 1 and 2 are categorized as not proficient. Levels 3 and 4 are proficient."[106] Therefore, third-grade reading proficiency is just 50%, and fourth-grade math proficiency is only 42%.

The board of education president, Joe Beveridge, was asked why Dr. Yeager's evaluation does not appear to include improvements in student achievement and if the district has a written plan to accomplish that objective. He did not respond.

Yeager is in the first year of a three-year deal that provides up to $312,000 annually, including $250,000 in base salary, up to a $25,000 bonus, a $25,000 contribution to a tax-deferred annuity, and a $12,000 car allowance. He also receives a health insurance allowance equal to the employee contribution for family coverage, KPERS retirement, and five weeks of vacation; he gets $1,033 for each unused vacation day.

Audit exposes academic shortcomings

The Kansas Division of Legislative Post Audit (LPA) released a limited-scope audit on March 7, 2022, to answer this question: What do stakeholders say about why developmental [remedial] college courses are necessary?[107]

The auditors sent surveys to 342 post-secondary instructors who teach developmental education courses, and 144 responded. They also sent surveys to 11,547 high school teachers, principals, and guidance counselors, and 1,559 responded.

The audit discloses that "a little more than 11,000 Kansas high school graduates were enrolled in at least one developmental education course" in the 2019–20 academic year (the year before COVID). That is about a third of all high school graduates in Kansas. And that only counts graduates who *enrolled* in a developmental education course. Considering that the state assessment test indicates that nearly three-quarters of the 2019 graduating class required some degree of remedial training, many more likely needed remedial training.[108] The 2019 ACT results also show low levels of college readiness. Only 27% of Kansas graduates who took the ACT were considered college-ready in English, reading, math, and science.[109]

LPA did not draw any conclusions or make recommendations, partly because the methodology did not qualify as a scientific survey. Still, the suggested evidence from anecdotal information should suffice to raise alarm bells.

Post-secondary survey respondents cited several significant factors prompting the need for developmental coursework. Students being out of high school for a considerable amount of time is the leading factor they cite, with 63% calling it a significant factor and 29% saying it is a minor factor. The other factors the audit cites directly reflect deficiencies in the public school system.

- The student is not a native English speaker and still needs language support—49% significant and 41% minor.
- The student did not take the appropriate coursework in high school—43% significant and 44% minor.
- High school content is not adequate to prepare students for college coursework—43% significant and 44% minor.
- State high school graduation requirements do not adequately prepare students for college—34% significant and 49% minor.

The high school survey respondents said the most critical factor was lack of educational support at home (69% significant, 28% minor). Their other observations are similar to post-secondary participants, although perhaps show even more damning concerns about the public school system.

- The student received passing grades without mastering the content—65% significant and 30% minor.
- The student did not take the appropriate coursework in high school—50% significant and 43% minor.

- The content of high school courses is not adequate to prepare students for college coursework—31% significant and 50% minor.
- The student had special needs that were not adequately addressed in high school—23% significant and 55% minor
- State high school graduation requirements do not adequately prepare students for college—20% significant and 47% minor.

High school staff also reported other opinions on why students are sometimes unprepared for college. Many respondents told auditors that academic expectations were too low in high school. One teacher wrote, "[I]t's not hard to pass with a 60%. That does not, however, make a student college-ready." Another noted that "grade inflation is rampant . . . the curriculum is watered down."

Many also noted that students struggle with basic skills when they enter high school. One teacher wrote, "students are being socially promoted in elementary schools and do not learn basic concepts."

The auditors interviewed other stakeholders about their opinions on why developmental education courses are necessary, including the Kansas Department of Education, the Kansas Association of Community Colleges, and the Kansas National Education Association. Every person they spoke with said a lack of appropriate high school coursework contributes to the need for developmental education coursework in college.

The audit findings are startling, but the reactions provide even more revealing insight into the public education system.

A letter from Blake Flanders, CEO of the Kansas Board of Regents, is included in the audit report. His thoughtful response mentions several steps KBOR is taking. The report also says KBOR generally agreed with the audit findings and conclusions.

The Kansas Department of Education had no comment. A response was not required because the audit did not make any recommendations, but the agency's silence speaks volumes.

Heidi Zimmerman, a principal auditor at Legislative Post Audit, presented the findings on March 7 to the House K–12 Budget Committee. Questions from legislators following her presentation also underscore the system's disregard for academic achievement. Legislators had advance copies of the audit, and the first few questions showed a concerted effort to dismiss the findings.

Representative Jarrod Ousley (D-Merriam) went first: "You said only 14% responded to the survey (1,559 out of 11,547 high school educators), but you sent out two surveys. Is that what I heard?"

Zimmerman said one survey went to high school educators and the other to post-secondary, which had a response rate of about 42%.

Ousley said, "I don't suppose we can draw any conclusions from the participation in the survey." Zimmerman agreed, and Ousley continued. "The 40% response rate from the secondary . . . is about average if I'm not mistaken."

Zimmerman said 30% to 40% is a pretty standard response rate, at which point responses are probably more representative of the larger group. Ousley then asked if there is a floor where, "you know, 14%, it's just not representative?"

Ousley had no questions about the findings; he just wanted them to go away.

Committee Chair Kristey Williams politely but firmly pushed back. "I would certainly not want to throw out the survey. They are simply a voluntary survey, and to ignore what 14% of teachers said would be a mistake, too. You might not be able to draw clear conclusions, but you can certainly draw clear conclusions on the 14% that responded."

The next question came from Rep. Valdenia Winn. Winn attempted to dismiss the audit findings on a timing basis. She noted the difference between the survey subjects who enrolled in college in the fall of 2019 and the survey going out in December 2021.

Rep. Stephanie Byers referenced the factor of students being out of high school for some time before enrolling in higher education, asking if the specific length of that time is known. Zimmerman said it was not.

The connection between the three efforts to dismiss the audit findings is that they have direct ties to the public education system. Ousley's wife is president of the Shawnee Mission School Board;[110] Winn serves on the Kansas City, Kansas, School District Board of Education;[111] and Byers is a retired teacher.[112]

The system defends the interests of the system and takes a "hear no evil, see no evil, speak no evil" approach, even with serious deficiencies staring it in the face. And this example from the developmental education audit is not a one-off; it is part of a pattern of behavior.

Chapter 4—School Officials Ignore State Law, Administrative Policy, and Legislative Intent

The Kansas State Department of Education says school districts "must be in good standing with KSDE regarding all applicable state and federal statutory and regulatory requirements" to be accredited.[113] The compliance document also defines "in good standing" as "in compliance, or actively working with the State Board to achieve compliance."

But much like a teenager learns that a curfew is just a suggestion if not enforced by parents, school officials have learned that complying with state statutory and regulatory requirements is optional, at least in terms of accreditation.

In 2019, for example, an audit examining how schools spend at-risk funding concluded that "most at-risk spending was used for teachers and programs for all students and did not appear to specifically address at-risk students as required by state law."

The legislature has provided more than $5 billion of additional funding since 2005 to improve outcomes for low-income students and those considered academically at risk. School districts receive at least $2,200 of extra funding for every student who meets the at-risk qualification; the most typical qualification is eligibility for free lunch.[114]

Kansas Legislative Division of Post Audit examined the practices of twenty school districts selected to "get a reasonable cross-section of school districts." One section of the audit report explained that most of the at-risk funding reviewed was spent on teachers and programs that serve all students rather than focusing on at-risk students.

> Based on state statute and KSDE (Kansas Department of Education) documents, at-risk funding is meant to provide at-risk students with additional educational opportunities and services to meet state educational outcomes. The department provides guidance to school districts, noting that these services should be "above and beyond" what is offered to all students.

Further, state law provides dedicated funding above the base state aid to help districts pay for these additional services.

For the 20 districts we reviewed, most at-risk funds were used for regular classroom teacher salaries. KSDE does not require teachers to track the amount of time they spend providing services to at-risk students. Instead, KSDE guidance allows districts to use at-risk funds to pay teacher salaries in proportion to the number of at-risk students. For example, if a school has 30% of students identified as at-risk, then 30% of classroom teacher salaries may be paid with at-risk funds.

All 20 districts reported they provide in-class assistance to their at-risk students. For example, breaking students into small groups based on skill level so that teachers can address specific needs. Additionally, many districts told us although these teachers teach all students in the classroom, they use programs and practices that are helpful for at-risk students. Last, based on what the districts and staff at KSDE told us, in-class assistance delivered by the regular classroom teacher is the primary way at-risk services are delivered to students.[115]

Even if the programs and practices are helpful, classroom instruction for all students is not providing services "above and beyond what is offered to all students." Auditors also found that only nine of the twenty-nine programs and practices districts said they were using "were specifically designed for at-risk students."

Other findings are equally disturbing:

- Only three of the twenty-nine programs and practices were proven to be effective.
- According to the WWC (What Works Clearinghouse), some of the most common programs districts told us they used for at-risk students had little to no effect on improving student outcomes.
- Many districts stated they used their at-risk funding to achieve smaller class sizes, but that practice has only limited success, according to several studies.

Requiring school districts to spend money based on "best practices" is better than nothing, but that still falls short of accountability. For example, nothing happened when schools were found not spending money as required by state law. Consequences that get the attention of education officials must exist for accountability measures to be effective.

The audit also notes that KSDE has not approved strong at-risk practices or given districts good guidance on at-risk spending.

These severe deficiencies prompted auditors to conclude that most school districts they examined "did not appear to specifically address at-risk students as required by state law."

The department of education and the state board of education disagreed that their approved programs and practices do not comply with state law, but the auditors stand by their conclusion for two reasons:

> State law requires that the approved programs and practices be for at-risk programs and for the instruction of at-risk students. The programs and practices the board has approved are not related to at-risk programs or students. Instead, the board has approved general teaching resources. The department has asserted that if a program or practice is good for all students, it is good for at-risk students. We do not think this view reflects what state law directs the board to do.
>
> State law requires the board to approve evidence-based programs and practices. The board asserted that every practice they have approved has been vetted by department staff. We asked to see this research, but department staff provided no evidence of a review. Additionally, the department's website did not provide any information on the research or evidence supporting the approved programs and practices. As a result, we concluded the board's approved programs and practices did not comply with this aspect of state law.

The state board of education's reaction to the at-risk audit is even more telling.

After a scathing editorial by the *Kansas City Star*, the state board of education president, Kathy Busch, wrote a response that essentially said, "Shut up, go away, we know what we're doing."[116]

Busch said the *Star* editorial "grossly misrepresents the hard work and careful appropriation of resources." The audit didn't examine whether people were working hard, but it carefully reviewed the misappropriation of funding concerning its compliance with state law.

Busch also said, "A fundamental flaw of the Legislative Post Audit report is that education research doesn't define best practices strictly, as is seen in many other fields. But Kansas schools are utilizing best practices."

Her statement is a classic tactic of the education establishment. First, she claims there isn't an exact definition to which schools can be held, and in the next breath, Busch says there *is* a standard, which is whatever schools happen to be doing.

Her indignant close reflects another standard tactic—bullying those who dare question the monarchy: "It is irresponsible and dangerous for others to oversimplify the magnitude of that task and the approaches we are taking to meet the needs of Kansas' at-risk students."

Busch offered nothing to substantiate how the state board of education meets student needs. And she couldn't because student achievement results and feedback from employers and colleges indicate otherwise.

If the state board and school districts were spending money effectively and following best practices, the results would reflect student achievement gains. Instead, race-based and income-based educational discrimination continue unabated.

The 2019 state audit was déjà vu all over again
The at-risk audit findings are certainly shocking but not surprising to insiders; the 2019 audit marked the *second* time school districts were found to not comply with at-risk procedures and spending intent.

In 2015, Kansas Policy Institute published a study by Senior Education Policy Analyst David Dorsey about a similar research project he conducted. Dorsey's analysis, however, examined the practices of all 286 school districts in Kansas.

School districts at that time had to submit an at-risk application and annual report to the department of education. The application explained how the district would spend its money, and the annual report described how services were provided.

Dorsey's review of the annual report revealed that at-risk dollars in many districts were used to help educate students who were not at-risk. He grouped his findings into four categories:

- **Specifically indicates funds to at-risk students only—** Only 34 districts described their services, making it clear that the at-risk funds were targeted only to those who were identified as being at-risk. DeSoto (USD 232) reported: "Our State At-Risk Funds are utilized to pay the salaries of teachers who serve at-risk students and provide at-risk (Tier 2 & Tier 3) interventions. These teachers would include reading specialists, ELL teachers, and one at-risk math teacher."

- **At-risk dollars used to serve non-at-risk students—**Some 120 districts described the use of at-risk funds—either directly or inferentially—that included reduction of class size or use a percentage of at-risk funds for teacher salaries. What Newton (USD 373) submitted is an example: "We provide bilingual/ESOL push-in/pull-out support; vocational career & technical education courses; preschool at-risk; full-day kindergarten for all students, and reduced class sizes in grades K–4."

- **Description not discernible/cannot classify—**The descriptions of 109 districts made it impossible to determine whether or not they were spending at-risk money to serve at-risk students. Here is the description provided by Central Heights (USD 288): "One to one support/assistance from teachers in all classes, after school tutoring, MTSS, STEM program, reading assistance program, reading recovery, summer school, classes added to the normal class schedule to provide academic support in reading and math."

- **Description did not match the 2014–15 budget**—The remaining 23 districts provided program descriptions for 2013–14 that were sufficiently different from their 2014–15 budget to warrant leaving them out of one of the other categories." [117]

The department of education at that time said the purpose of its Kansas At-Risk Pupil Assistance Program was "to provide at-risk students with additional educational opportunities and instructional services to assist in closing the achievement gap."

But the gaps grew wider, as seen in Figure 9. For example, the income-based achievement gap in NAEP reading proficiency was 22 percentage points in 2005. It gradually became worse over the next ten years, and in 2015, the gap was 34 percentage points.

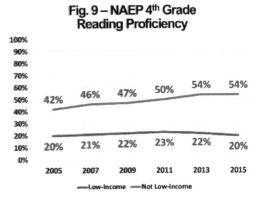

Fig. 9 – NAEP 4ᵗʰ Grade Reading Proficiency

The gap in eighth-grade reading proficiency widened from 22 points to 25 points. In math, the gap held steady in fourth grade but was worse in eighth grade. Achievement gaps also grew worse on the state assessment.

The NAEP proficiency gaps persist today, as noted earlier in Table 10.

The department of education implemented a new state assessment program in 2015, with changes sufficient to render comparisons to prior assessments invalid. That said, the race-based and income-based gaps remain pretty significant. For example, low-income students are twice as likely to be below grade level in math (48% vs. 25%), while their more affluent peers are twice as likely to be proficient (37% vs. 15%).

The 2019 audit prompted the legislature to add an accountability measure to ensure that money would be allocated to close achievement gaps. But education officials are ignoring it as well.

Education officials ignore state law that requires building needs assessments
For more than twenty years, local school boards have been statutorily required to annually conduct assessments to determine the educational needs of each attendance center in the district. The law directs school boards to use the information obtained when preparing the district budget.[118]

As mentioned previously, school districts have repeatedly sued the State of Kansas, claiming to be underfunded. The last time the Kansas Supreme Court ordered additional funding, it said having about a quarter of students tested below grade level somehow proved that funding was inadequate.[119] But absent a requirement that funding be used for that specific purpose, legislators feared it was only a matter of time before the schools went back for more money under the same pretense.

So they amended the building needs assessment language in 2021 accordingly (the new language is italicized):

> Each year the board of education of a school district shall conduct an assessment of the educational needs of each attendance center in the district. Information obtained from such needs assessment shall be used by the board when preparing the budget of the school district *to ensure improvement in student academic performance. The budget of the school district shall allocate sufficient moneys in a manner reasonably calculated such that all students may achieve the goal set forth in K.S.A. 72-3218(c), and amendments thereto.*[120]

"To ensure improvement" was always the intent, but the phrase was added to prevent education officials from feigning misunderstanding if they sued again. The goals referenced in K.S.A. 72-3218(c) are specific capacities identified by the court.

The hope was that education officials would allocate their budgets to improve achievement. If not, the new language helps the legislature defend against another lawsuit claiming inadequate funding to educate students.

The new language went into effect with the 2021 school budget cycle. Afterward, Kansas Policy Institute filed a series of Open Records requests with twenty-five of the largest school districts to audit their compliance and gauge the impact of the new language.

Unfortunately (but not surprisingly), the audit disclosed a general disregard for the law and its intent.

Two districts—Coffeyville and Kansas City—completed the forms recommended by the department of education, but the two most important questions are missing and therefore unanswered. Neither district identified any specific barrier to improving achievement or what budget priorities would be adjusted accordingly. The audit also discovered glaringly inadequate information, indicating a disregard for the exercise's purpose.

The Coffeyville Elementary School report says 36 of its 940 students enrolled last year were not proficient; that is roughly 4%. But 88% are not proficient, according to the Kansas Department of Education state assessment results.[121]

The Roosevelt Middle School and Field Kindley High School reports are also grossly inaccurate. The needs assessments say 16% and 12%, respectively, are not proficient. But the state assessment shows 77% and 93%, respectively, are not proficient.[122]

There is little hope that these needs assessments will inform the budget process when the reports grossly understate students' academic needs. It's also telling that the question about disparities in student achievement among ethnic groups is left blank on each report.

The Kansas City, Kansas, district utilizes similar reports to those in Coffeyville. And like Coffeyville, Kansas City identifies very little information that could inform the budget process about improving student achievement. They also grossly mispresent student achievement in the district. The report doesn't say how many students are not proficient in math and English language arts; it merely links to the state assessment results. The comments are even more deceptive.[123]

The math comment on the F. L. Schlagle High School report says, "10th Grade PLC has created plans to help students understand what is being asked in the Math problem. They emphasize scholarly language." The ELA section says, "10th Grade ELA has shown growth. PLC practices are improving."[124]

The state assessment results show that 3% of Schlagle students are proficient in math and only 6% in ELA. How are students expected to understand "scholarly language" when 63% of them can't read at grade level?[125] Kansas City completed a report for each attendance center, but each amounts to nothing more than going through the motions with regard to improving student achievement.

Five other districts defiantly ignored the statutory requirement. Three of them—Shawnee Mission, Blue Valley, and Gardner-Edgerton—took the position that the statute doesn't specify a written report, so they had no records responsive to the Open Records request.

Gardner-Edgerton hired outside counsel to respond to the Open Records request. Grant Tideman of Lathrop and Gage wrote, "USD 231 has no documents responsive to this request. Your request seems to assume that there is a legal requirement for a specific written form to be prepared and retained by USD 231. If so, I disagree with that assumption. There is no legal requirement for such a specific written form."

David Smith, chief communications officer at Shawnee Mission, said the information from the assessments was shared verbally with board members, but that begs credulity. It is preposterous to claim that a large volume of information obtained from visiting forty-four school buildings was effectively conveyed to school board members without writing anything on paper. But that is typical of some school officials.

Garden City Financial Officer Colleen Drees wrote, "Garden City Public Schools (USD 457) does a building needs assessment (assessment) for each attendance center, every year, as required by K.S.A. 72-1163. The district does the assessments through meetings, committees, and updates with department heads. The assessments are then used by the board of education to prepare the annual budget and summary of the budget, both of which are written documents required by K.S.A. 72-1163. The aforementioned statute does not require a written assessment document. Therefore, the requested records do not exist. USD 457 is not required under KORA to create a record that does not previously exist."

Drees said the assessments were discussed at the board meetings on July 12, July 26, and August 23, but there is no mention of that occurring in the agendas or meeting minutes.

The Iola school district demanded $377 in advance to have several administrators search their records to see if they have the requested reports. An Open Records complaint was filed with the Allen County Attorney, who never responded to the complaint.

The remaining eighteen districts sent various documents, but nothing indicating that they conducted the statutorily required building needs assessment. Conversations with officials in those districts made it clear that some were unfamiliar with the requirement.

Teachers routinely say they have no input on properly allocating resources to improve outcomes and close race-based and income-based educational discrimination.

Garry Sigle is the executive director of the Kansas Association of American Educators, a statewide non-union, professional educators' organization. He says teachers work hard to meet the standards but aren't consulted by administrators: "I think there are a lot of times that the administration comes around with the newest fad. Again, I'm basing this [on] my experience in the classroom. They come around with the newest educational fad, and sometimes I think educators just kind of roll their eyes like okay, well, what is it this time?"[126]

The findings of KPI's audit prompted corrective measures to be proposed in Senate Bill 362 during the 2022 legislative session.[127]

- Each building needs assessment report must be posted on district websites.
- The meeting minutes at which the board approves its annual budget must include that the needs assessment reports were provided to the board, that the board evaluated the reports, and explain how the information informed the budget process.
- The assessment report must identify the barriers to be overcome so that all students can perform at least at grade

level on the state assessment. They must also specify the budgetary actions that should be taken to remove such barriers and the amount of time it will take for all students to perform at grade level if those budget actions are implemented.

The Senate Education Committee held a hearing on SB 362 on February 10, 2022. Mark Tallman, representing the Kansas Association of School Boards, testified neutral on the bill. He said KASB's interpretation of the existing law is that "the existing law has never required a particular process or a particular needs assessment.[128] Tallman said that if the goal was to have a record of the process, that that should be made clear.

Senator Molly Baumgartner took issue with his interpretation.

You indicated in your testimony that . . . if we want something from our boards of education, we're going to have to make it clear. I'm going to read specifically from the statute. "Each year, the board of education of a school district shall conduct an assessment for the educational needs of each attendance center in the district."

I don't know what could be more clear than that. They must conduct it. I assume if they conduct it, they are documenting it in some way. Are you saying it doesn't have to be published and KORA [Open Records] ready? Is that what your position is?

Tallman repeated his interpretation in response—that no particular instrument is required to be used. Baumgardner said the revised law passed in 2021 is very clear.

Show your work. Show it so we can see at a building level how the budget was built for any given district. Did you really pay attention to how many students are attending classes, how many students are at-risk? We know that changes from year to year, but we haven't seen anything in writing to indicate that the school districts are actually doing that.

So I want to understand really where you're coming from because right now, it is still standing like, "OK, if you guys want it, you're going to have to be really specific before we're going to deliver it."

Quite frankly, I think what I've heard from constituents, from teachers, from parents, and from other legislators is "When is our public education community going to come together and start helping solve the issues?"

So here we are, a year later, and school districts are saying to us by your testimony, is "Well, we just haven't figured out how to do that yet." So we're going to find a way to figure it out, and we will document it in legislation. And so be it if the legislators have to come up with the building assessments, then we will.

Senator Rene Erickson also expressed her displeasure with KASB's dog-ate-my-homework excuse.

Frankly, I'm frustrated that we have a law that's very clear, and what we get from the people who are supposed to be teaching our children critical thinking skills are telling us they can't comply with the law because, well, let me tell you what I heard today.

"We're too busy . . . we don't have a set format . . . we don't have enough money . . . we're already doing it."

Madam Chair, I'm with (you). I am happy to put that in place. It wouldn't be hard to put that in place. But I guarantee what we'll hear is, "That's the local control, that's the responsibility of the local school board." I would just like to know what we are to do when local school boards aren't complying with the law, and then this is the response we get when we try to make sure that that law is enforced for a very good reason.

Why wouldn't we want to base our allocation of funds on what's best for kids? I read what the requirements are, and I'm like, "Why on earth is that such a hard lift?" And the only thing I can think of quite frankly is, "You can't make us, and you can't tell us what to do." And I find that quite shocking, Madam Chair.

Fortunately for students, the new provisions are now ensconced in state law. The contents of SB 362 were folded into another bill—Senate Substitute for House Bill 2567. The senate approved it by a 24–14 vote, and the house approved it on a 75–45 vote.

Governor Kelly's Commission on Racial Equity & Justice ignores educational discrimination

You might think that a commission formed to study "issues of racial equity and justice in Kansas" would take a hard look at educational discrimination, especially with two educators co-chairing the commission.[129] But you would be wrong.

Kansas Governor Laura Kelly appointed Dr. Tiffany Anderson, superintendent of the Topeka School District, and Dr. Shannon Portillo, associate dean of Academic Affairs at the University of Kansas Edwards Campus, to co-chair the commission. The superintendent of the Lawrence School District, Dr. Anthony Lewis, was also appointed to the commission. It is hard to imagine other commission members ignoring race-based educational discrimination if those educators brought it to their attention.

The report cites statistics about earnings gaps for people of color and blithely attributes it to "lower rates of enrollment in and completion of postsecondary degree programs." The only rationale offered for lower enrollment is money-related, as in, students of color who graduate have much higher levels of student debt. But maybe, just maybe, the fact that most Black and Hispanic high school students are below grade level has something to do with them not obtaining a postsecondary education. And perhaps the fact that this is a systemic, generational problem explains why their parents are less able to afford college and career training.

The 2021 state assessment results show that White students are two to three times more likely than students of color to be on track for college and career, and the high school results are worse. On the ACT, only 5% of Black graduates were college-ready in English, reading, math, and science, compared to 25% of White students. These deplorable results come as no surprise to educators; after all, the National Assessment of Educational Progress shows Black fourth graders in Kansas are 2.6 years' worth of learning behind White students.

So why would Governor Kelly's commission fail to address blatant educational discrimination in the Kansas public school system? Quite simply, doing so means admitting that a problem exists and education officials won't follow state laws designed to close achievement gaps. And the first commandment of Kansas politics is "Thou shalt not criticize the public education system." The education system delivers a lot of votes to those who do its bidding; those who don't will feel its wrath.

The only recommendations that the commission report relates to achievement are things like hiring more teachers of color, making it easier for minorities to become teachers, and giving more money to districts with high-need students. That last one should read, "The legislature provided over $5 billion in incremental at-risk funding since 2005, so follow the damn law and use it as intended."

Like the Governor's Tax Council, this commission was designed to provide cover for pre-determined political positions. The Tax Commission paved the way to use the state tax code to redistribute wealth with what it defined as vertical equity.

Vertical equity is based on the premise that those who earn more money or have more economic resources should be taxed at higher rates than those earning less income and having fewer economic resources. Vertical equity promotes proportional or progressive taxes where tax as a share of income increases as income increases [and] those with a greater ability should pay more.[130]

Of course, Kansas already had "vertical equity." Data from the Kansas Department of Revenue for Tax Year 2019 shows that people with more than $250,000 in Adjusted Gross Income accounted for 27% of AGI and paid 31% of income tax. Every AGI bracket above $75,000 paid a higher share of taxes than its share of total AGI, and every bracket below that level paid a smaller share relative to the percentage of AGI. Those with the highest AGI also paid a higher effective tax rate (ETR). Taxpayers with AGI below $50,000 paid an effective tax rate of 1.8%, while those over $100,000 AGI paid an ETR of 4%.[131]

But the facts don't matter when trying to justify a tax increase. That desire to further shift the tax burden to those with higher incomes makes an appearance in the final report of the Commission on Racial Equity & Justice.

Instead of tackling race-based educational discrimination head-on, the commission recommends several tax burden shifts, including "an additional bracket for high income [*sic*] earners in the state to a more equitable tax structure."

Giving students the education they need to be successful in life is the way to address income equality, boost self-esteem, reduce dependence on social services, and keep people out of the prison system. But that doesn't fit the political agenda, so the commission ignored it.

Department guidance and legislative intent are ignored

The Kansas Supreme Court in 2005 ordered the legislature to increase school funding by $853 million in *Montoy v. State of Kansas*, opining that the legislature was not meeting its obligation to fund schools constitutionally. The legislature modified the school funding formula to satisfy the court, but it also passed a policy position to provide direction on spending the windfall.

The history of school finance litigation from the perspective of students and taxpayers could be a book in itself. Still, a brief background helps explain the legislature's thinking on its policy position.

The *Montoy* court relied on a cost study by Augenblick & Myers (A&M) to reach its $853 million decision. But subsequent analysis showed that A&M ignored its own methodology in arriving at its recommendation. Caleb Stegall, then a legal scholar with Kansas Policy Institute and now a state supreme court justice, authored a legal analysis of *Montoy* in 2009.[132]

The legislature tasked the Legislative Education Planning Committee (LEPC) with hiring a firm to conduct a study "to determine the cost, both per pupil and additional costs, of providing a suitable education 'in typical K–12 schools of various sizes and locations.'"[133] The LEPC contracted with Augenblick & Myers.

A&M based its findings on the Successful Schools Approach, which is described as determining "a base cost by looking at the actual spending by districts that already meet the suitable education standard."

But that is not what they did, as Stegall explains:

> A&M emphasized that some of the strengths of the successful schools approach were its ability to identify a base cost figure, and "that it allows for the inclusion of spending efficiency to be used as a measure of success." Regarding the latter, A&M had hoped to further winnow the number of "successful school" district models by examining the efficiency with which the 85 districts spent their money. After analyzing how several factors (such as attendance center size, enrollment, proportion of low-income students, and local tax effort) affected spending, A&M used these results to estimate a "predicted spending" efficiency level for each district. A&M then compared this "predicted spending" level for each district to a district's actual spending, seeking to identify which school districts were spending efficiently. But when the results demonstrated that 50 of the 85 "successful school" districts would be considered inefficient spenders, A&M decided not to use efficiency as a component of a "successful school," choosing instead to use all 85 school districts. A&M concluded that had it used efficiency standard to exclude those 50 districts, this "might [have] undermine[d] the possibility that this higher [albeit inefficient] spending is what allows districts to be successful in Kansas." In other words, as throughout the cost-study process, methodologies were adopted expressly because of the results they could be expected to deliver.[134]

According to Mike O'Neal, the *Montoy* decision also ignored established Kansas Supreme Court precedent in ordering a funding increase. He references the court's 1994 opinion in *U.S.D. No. 229 v. State*, where the court said: "[T]he issue is whether (the School District Finance and Quality Performance Act) satisfies the constitution by providing suitable financing, not whether the level of finance is optimal or the best policy."[135]

Article 6, Section 6(b), of the Kansas Constitution says, "The legislature shall make suitable provision for finance of the educational interests of the state. No tuition shall be charged for attendance at any public school to pupils required by law to attend such school, except such fees or supplemental charges as may be authorized by law."[136]

The court's 1994 opinion said the constitution merely requires a finance system, such as a formula. That is reinforced in the second sentence of Section 6(b), which essentially says, "and don't include tuition in the formula."

Despite all of this, the *Montoy* court arguably violated the Separation of Powers doctrine and ordered the legislative branch of government to increase school funding by $853 million. The court also ignored a constitutional provision specifying that appropriating money is the exclusive province of the legislature. Article 2, Section 24, says, "Appropriations. No money shall be drawn from the treasury except in pursuance of a specific appropriation made by law.[137]

Against this backdrop, the 2005 legislature passed a policy position calling on schools to allocate 65% of total spending to Instruction.[138] The reference to "Instruction" is based on the *Department of Kansas Accounting Handbook* guidance. It tells school districts that Instruction spending—direct interaction between teachers and students—is "the most important part of the education program, the very foundation on which everything else is built. If this function fails to perform at the needed level, the whole educational program is doomed to failure regardless of how well the other functions perform."[139]

The other expense functions are Student Support, Staff Support, Administration, Operations & Maintenance, Transportation, Food Service, Capital Outlay, Debt Services, and Other.[140]

School districts collectively allocated 54.2% of total spending to Instruction during the 2005 school year, including Capital Outlay money for instructional purposes.[141] Figure 10 shows a slight gradual decline in the Instruction allocation since then, to 52.6% for the 2021 school year.

If local school boards acted in accordance with the legislature's 65% recommendation, $10 billion more would have been spent on Instruction since 2005. Even if administrators and local school boards increased their Instruction allocation by just a half percentage point each year, they would have spent $4.2 billion more on Instruction through the 2021 school year. Spending on everything else would still have increased by 41% and grown faster than inflation.[142]

Education officials essentially thumb their noses at the legislature, department of education spending guidance, and most importantly, students, when they continually allocate barely half of all spending to the function that matters most to student outcomes. The schools' argument that no research says 65% or any other allocation is ideal is valid. But officials blithely ignore the essence of the legislature's policy goal of using the funding windfall in students' best interests. And it is not as though their approach is proving beneficial to students.

Fig. 10: Per-Student Spending Allocation

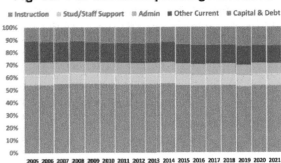

While local school boards and administrators generally continue following the same spending patterns repeatedly, their actions have not produced better outcomes. Throughout this book, student achievement is shown to be down or flat over the last twenty years and remains quite low. Only 21% of Kansas graduates who took the 2021 ACT were considered college-ready in English, reading, math, and science. The 2021 state assessment shows Kansas has more high school students below grade level than are proficient and on track for college and career.

Districts' disregard for their legal obligations and spending guidance also perpetuated educational discrimination. In 2005, low-income fourth graders were 2.2 years' worth of learning behind their more affluent peers in reading on the National Assessment of Educational Progress (NAEP). They were 2.7 years behind in 2019, and their proficiency level was flat at 20%. Low-income eighth graders also lost ground. They went from 2.1 years behind to 2.3 years behind, and proficiency fell from 21% to 19%.

All external factors, especially the student achievement data and education officials' public actions, indicate no serious effort to end educational discrimination. If anything, Kansans Can and the school redesign project makes it worse. And the system-over-students attitude is also apparent to insiders.

Chapter 5—The Public Education Governance System Works against Students

Kansas became the thirty-fourth state in 1861, and the Wyandotte Constitution officially became the Constitution of the State of Kansas. The Kansas Office of the Revisor of Statutes gave the legislature a brief history of changes to the education provisions in 2017:

Article 6, Section 1 of the Wyandotte Constitution vested an elected state superintendent of public instruction with general supervision of school funds and the educational interests of the state. Section 2 required the Legislature to "encourage the promotion of intellectual, moral, scientific and agricultural improvement by establishing a uniform system of common schools, and schools of a higher grade." Section 3 concerned proceeds from certain land sales and estates which must be applied to schools. Section 4 provided that state school funds be disbursed annually to county treasurers then disbursed to school districts "in equitable proportion to the number of children and youth resident therein." Section 5 related to the sale and lease of school lands. Section 6 concerned moneys that must be applied to the state school fund. Section 7 required the Legislature to establish a "State University, for the promotion of literature and the arts and sciences, including a normal and agricultural department." Section 8 prohibited any religious sect or sects from controlling school funds. Section 9 vested the management and investment of school funds in a board of commissioners which consisted of the State Superintendent, the Secretary of State, and the Attorney General. Section 10, which was ratified in 1918, authorized the Legislature to levy a permanent tax for the state educational institutions.

As the state's educational system progressed beyond the educational system that was contemplated during territorial times, the Legislature implemented statutory changes to meet and keep up with modern educational demands. A few examples of these statutory changes include: Expanding the constitutional one university system into a system of three universities; statutorily creating a state board of education and a state board of regents; creating high school districts; undertaking a comprehensive study of education in the late 1950s; passing the 1963 school unification act which reduced the number of school districts from 1,745 districts to 380 districts; and in 1965, expanding state aid to public schools by establishing a foundation finance plan to help localities finance education requirements.

Despite those changes, the Legislature recognized that more changes were still needed to replace the inherited educational system with a system that was more reflective of modern conditions. In the 1965 regular legislative session, the Legislature passed House Concurrent Resolution 537 directing the Kansas Legislative Council to study "the scope, function, and organization of the state in supervising education" and "the education article of the constitution and any needed amendments thereto."

The Kansas Legislative Council appointed an Education Advisory Committee to assist with the comprehensive study of the education article of the constitution. The Education Advisory Committee was composed of eleven prominent citizens of Kansas. The major recommendations by the Education Advisory Committee included: completely rewriting the education article of the Kansas Constitution to provide a new framework for present and future educational requirements; providing for a constitutional state board of regents and state board of education; placing responsibility of public education below the college level with the state board of education; and giving the legislature greater flexibility in educational finance. The Education Advisory Committee's report proposed new constitutional language for the education article to effectuate its recommendations. On November 9, 1965, the Education Advisory Committee submitted its report to the Kansas Legislative Council for consideration.[143]

According to the Education Commission of the States, Kansas is one of only seven states with this education governance system, which it calls Model Two—a majority or all of the state board of education members are elected, and the board appoints the chief state school officer.[144] The other states are Alabama, Colorado, Louisiana, Michigan, Nebraska, and Utah.

ECS says forty-one of the fifty states fall into one of four governance structures, and the other nine states fall into modified versions of the four general models. The other three models are:

- Model One—the governor appoints the majority or all members of the state board of education, which, in turn, selects the chief state school officer.
- Model Three—the governor appoints the majority or all state board of education members, and the chief state school officer is elected.
- Model Four—the governor appoints the majority or all members of the state board of education and the chief state school officer.

These three models have one crucial thing in common—the governor is responsible and can much more easily be held accountable for student performance. Voters in these states need only change the course of one statewide election to demand improvement. But there are ten state school board members in Kansas with staggered terms, so voters must win and hold at least six races over an extended period to effect change. These races represent ten different regions, elected by the voters of each area. Simply put, the education governance model in Kansas is itself a barrier to better educational outcomes.

Elected state school board members tend to act like many other elected officials, as economist Thomas Sowell explains: "No one will really understand politics until they understand that politicians are not trying to solve our problems. They are trying to solve their own problems—of which getting elected and re-elected are number one and number two. Whatever is number three is far behind."[145]

To get elected and re-elected, state school board members must satisfy those who have the most influence in getting them elected. In Kansas, that is the education bureaucracy, not parents. Teacher unions, the state association of school boards, superintendents, and a host of state and local political organizations have one primary interest—money.

They want state school board members who will advocate for more school funding and be cheerleaders for the system, or at least not get in the way. The bureaucracy runs the system, and the role of state board members is to support the bureaucracy. Student achievement is to be given lip service and nothing else. Just advocate for more money.

The July 2016 state board of education meeting is a perfect example of the blind devotion to funding, as documented by KPI scholar David Dorsey:[146]

The way in which the board came to this decision bordered on the surreal. Each year the Board is required by law to make budget recommendations to the governor for the upcoming (two) fiscal years. At the July meeting, Deputy KSDE Commissioner Dale Dennis led the Board through the process by providing budget recommendations in 17 different categories.[147]

It is quite apparent from watching the proceedings that the Board made this decision hastily with little or no thought to the consequences of their actions. KPI also learned pursuant to a KORA (Kansas Open Records Act) request that no communication between KSDE staff and the State Board was made prior to the meeting. According to Scott Gordon, General Counsel for KSDE, he was told by agency staff that "there was no email or communication between KSDE and Board members other than the Board packet that's available on the KSDE website" with reference to the budget recommendations.

The $900 million increase was approved on a 7–3 vote, opposed by Ken Willard, Steve Roberts and John Bacon. The increase is based on raising base state aid per pupil (BSAPP) to $4,650 for 2017–18 and bumping it up to $5,150 in 2018–19. Those options were chosen from a list of seven choices for 2017–18 and eight for 2018–19 that were presented to the Board by Mr. Dennis. The Board discussed it for less than 20 minutes before approving it, with hardly a word about where the money would come from to pay for it. More importantly, there was no discussion of how (or whether) another $900 million would close achievement gaps or improve overall outcomes.[148]

At the time, the legislature was providing about $4 billion in funding for public education, with total funding at $6.1 billion.[149] A budget recommendation of this magnitude should take weeks of review. State school board members should be grilling department of education officials on the need for additional funding, the effectiveness of money spent in prior years, and how the additional funding would improve student achievement. Instead, board members (or at least seven) simply approved the proposal in less than twenty minutes.

No cooperation with the legislature
State board members may profess a desire to work with the legislature toward better outcomes, but it's mostly posturing for the media. Truth be told, the state board of education treats the legislature with contempt and condescension.

The 2021 legislature approved two bills requiring students to pass civics and financial literacy tests to graduate. But the state board of education considered that reasonable legislation as an act of war.

As reported by the *Kansas City Star*, "Gov. Laura Kelly says education is none of the Legislature's business—that it's the exclusive province of the duly elected Kansas State Board of Education. So she vetoed the bills.[150]

The state board of education held a lengthy conversation at its June 2021 meeting about the perceived intrusion on its turf. The merit of requiring high school students to pass tests on civics and financial literacy before graduating wasn't even a passing thought. It was all about establishing dominion over the legislature.

Kansas State Board President Jim Porter said, "I really think that it's time for us to make a definitive statement."[151]

Board member Janet Waugh said she understood that the state board of education is "almost a fourth branch of government."[152]

That an elected official would even think that the state board of education is the fourth branch of government only underscores the need for having students pass a civics test. But the state board is only interested in its authority, not its responsibility to see that every student is academically prepared for college or career.

The board decided to draft a statement on its authority that would be polite but "unambiguous and non-negotiable."

There was talk of having a series of meetings with the legislature ahead of the 2022 session about "partnering" on issues. Still, House K–12 Budget Chair Kristey Williams provides another example that indicates the lack of sincerity on the board's part: "I'm still waiting for the state board to engage on third-grade literacy. That's something we talked about in November 2021. It was something that our interim committee took an interest in and invited the state board to participate. And I've yet to hear any discussions. No questions or suggestions from the state board relating to that. So considering they have not responded . . . I would say they're not as interested in achievement as the legislature."[153]

Former Speaker of the House Mike O'Neal says the department of education and the state board have been very uncooperative. "They have tried to take the position that it's none of the legislature's business; they've got everything under control. 'Nothing to see here; just keep moving on.' And yet, with all the transparency pieces we've put in place, we can watch every dollar and all the assessment scores. We know that things aren't as good as what the department is trying to make it. And then, when we try to enact some reforms that will actually help Johnny and Susie learn something, we get nothing but pushback from the department."[154]

Williams says there is minimal discussion of substance from the state board and the department about improving weak academic performance, let alone honestly acknowledging the existence of a severe problem. "It's the state board that determines and approves the standards. They are the ones that determine the benchmarks. When [so many] students cannot get to the state benchmarks since 2015, then what we hear are excuses. Certainly, we can measure outcomes in multiple ways, but this should be the basic one. And you know, we shouldn't have 72% of our kids not proficient in math.

That doesn't make sense."[155]

Williams references the 2021 state assessment results for all students tested in grades three through eight and ten: "I think that there's a natural inclination to avoid tough topics. And so, I think that's certainly a reality. I think there's also a natural inclination to protect the schools because we do have some pretty amazing students and teachers, and we don't want to undermine the good work that has been accomplished. But at the same time, we shouldn't be fearful to look at ways to improve and just to talk honestly about it."[156]

O'Neal is blunter in his assessment: "I would say that the education establishment really doesn't respect the legislature. They would like the legislature to stay out of their business and are not fully cooperating with efforts on the part of the legislature to get information and try to develop policy that's going to make a difference in terms of outcomes."[157]

The state's education governance model emboldens the bureaucracy. There is no incentive to improve or be responsive to the legislature, with no single individual who can ultimately be held accountable for resolving educational discrimination and other challenges.

Legislators likely wouldn't be pushing the department and the state board if they met their goals, like having 75% proficiency in math and reading. But the legislature has become increasingly engaged over the last few years as the bureaucracy's disinformation campaign has been exposed.

The media aided and abetted the deception over the years. The capitol press corps has been particularly antagonistic toward the legislature, to the point of being, as O'Neal says, apologists for the education community. He says that has a lot to do with politics—the legislature is conservative, and the media is not conservative-leaning—but the situation is shifting.

"I'm seeing some evidence this year, where the media has sort of woken up to the fact that despite unprecedented levels of funding—and levels of funding that meet constitutional mandates—that outcomes are still lagging behind," O'Neal said.

The Kansas Constitution grants no authority to district administrators, but O'Neal says superintendents routinely exert influence over school board members. "We're hearing anecdotally that [school board members] are being advised to just go along with the administration when it comes to the budget. The Kansas Constitution does not give the administration any power. All the power resides in the local school boards. The overall duty to supervise is with the state board of education. There's nothing in the Constitution that says the administration has control over anything; they can advise."[158]

Former Louisburg School Board member Douglas Shane says some superintendents may *say* they work for the school board, but reality is much different. In his opinion, the Kansas Association of School Boards tells new board members just to support the superintendent. "Kind of how they train new school board members and everything is that they basically say, 'Well, you're not actually there to do much of anything of impact or importance. You really need to listen to your superintendents and receive guidance on things that need to be done for the school.'" [159]

Shane says many new board members come into office not knowing much about the operation of a school district and tend to rely on administrators for guidance.

> They tend to be very trusting of those unelected people who work in the district. And so they don't know what they don't know. And they don't necessarily have a firm vision for the direction they want to take the school district, and they don't know how to—even if they have a vision—they don't know how to achieve it. They don't understand how the laws work. What's actually the ramification of policy? What does it mean when a school board sets policy? And all of those kinds of things.
>
> So, you know, school boards kind of get in their own way because they don't understand; they don't understand their own authority and their own ability to influence what happens in the district.
>
> Now, on top of that, over the last decades, there has also been intentionality between all government entities, which are run by the unelected, in that they try to subvert the authority of the elected, and they do that through lies of omission,

misdirection, lack of transparency, and you know, and other methodologies to kind of hold on to their own power and authority and actually many times they get the elected to cede their authority to them.[160]

Shane shared an example to make his point: the Louisburg School Board decided not to use COVID relief money to give bonuses to teachers, thinking it was not an appropriate use of the funds. Shortly after that, District Superintendent Brian Biermann "got an earful" from State Superintendent Randy Watson, who said the department of education wanted districts to pay teacher bonuses with the COVID money.

Watson has no authority over local school boards' spending decisions, and school superintendents do not work for the department of education. But Biermann went back to Louisburg and "basically told the board 'this is what I'm going to do.'"

"We never actually put it to a vote (to rescind the vote to not pay bonuses)," Shane said, "and we never discussed it in public forum. He unilaterally made the choice and made the spend."

Shane also says there is considerable pressure put on school board members not to speak up in the community. "There is immense pressure to never say anything, never to rebuke the school in any way, to say that you're doing anything wrong, to call a teacher that needs to be held accountable to the table. As a matter of fact, I got lectured in a public meeting that my role was not to question. Basically, I was lectured by another board member, that I was exceeding the role of a school board member, and it's not our job to actually run the school district."

School boards defend district officials by shutting down public comments

Instead of representing parents' interests, some local school board members shield district officials from parental concerns.

Although not required by law, school board meetings have traditionally included a public forum session to allow parents and other community members to address the board. These sessions are called forums but are not the typical exchanges of ideas and views in an actual forum. Board members and the superintendent most often just listen but say nothing as a matter of policy. For example, board members in the Manhattan-Ogden School District are severely restricted by policy: "Except to ask clarifying questions, board members shall not interact with speakers at the open forum."[161]

Policies of this nature are contrived to prevent district officials and school board members from dealing with issues on the record. They also arguably violate the free speech rights of elected school board members who want to discuss a concern in public.

Speakers are given two or three minutes to speak and then asked to sit down.

Some school boards adopt policies to make it difficult for parents to obtain a slot on the agenda. Kansas City, Kansas, for example, requires parents to submit their request to speak by noon the day before a board meeting.[162] They also hold board meetings at 5:00 p.m. and open the forum early in the session, precluding many working parents from attending.

Most school boards prohibit speakers from criticizing individual board members or employees, but in at least one school district— Shawnee Mission—board members are permitted to make false accusations of speakers.

I was the first speaker at the public forum for the district's property tax and budget hearing on August 23, 2021. Board president Heather Ousley interrupted my introduction to allow another board member, Mary Sinclair, to make a statement.[163]

"I would just ask whether our guest would indicate whether you're speaking as a resident or on behalf of the organization for which you are a paid lobbyist that advocates for vouchers and lower school funding for Shawnee Mission in our public schools or in some other capacity."

Speakers always indicate whether they are speaking on behalf of an organization; it's required in the rules. The purpose of Sinclair's interruption was to make a false accusation and "discredit the witness," which I quickly noted.

I'll be happy to do that, and I'll start by correcting your false statement about what I do and what we stand for.

I am with Kansas Policy Institute, and I am the CEO. We advocate for better education opportunities for all students because unfortunately in Kansas, we have more high school students below grade level, according to the Kansas Department of Education, than are on track for college and career. Right here in Shawnee Mission, a third of the high school students are below grade level. That's according to the department of education.

We are not advocating to reduce funding. I don't know where you get that, but that's what some people say when they don't want the truth to come out about student achievement. Now, if I could, I'll go into my comments.

The Olathe school district restricts access to public comments at its meetings by holding the "public forum" immediately preceding the official board meeting. They don't broadcast and record the public forum, so most residents have no idea that patrons are raising serious and valid concerns with the board.

The May 5, 2022, public forum is a good example. Olathe business owner Rebecca Shipley questioned the ethical basis for giving Superintendent Brent Yeager a bonus when teachers, aides, and paras have lost jobs, and academic scores are down. She also objected to the grounds for awarding a bonus.

> Correct me if I have been misinformed, but I understand that our superintendent will be receiving a bonus based solely on the implementation of social programs such as DEI and not on academic achievement.[164]

As reported earlier in this book, Shipley's understanding of the basis for awarding a bonus is mainly correct. Yeager's bonus isn't solely based on DEI implementation—there are four other non-academic criteria—but the essence of her concern is valid and accurate.

Olathe school board president Joe Beveridge didn't respond to Ms. Shipley at the board meeting or subsequently, but he falsely accused her of misinformation in emails to others who shared her concerns:

It's somewhat ironic that you bring up the fact that you did not know the reference made during our regular meeting regarding one of the community member's public comments. In this case, the community member made a false statement that was 100 percent incorrect about Dr. Yeager. This is one of the many reasons I am against live-streaming public comments; misinformation is shared on a regular basis and this ends up costing our staff members time correcting the misinformation and not doing the job running the school district.[165]

Beveridge consciously deceived parents about the basis for Yeager's bonus, and he used misinformation to disparage Ms. Shipley while preposterously purporting to be preventing misinformation. And he's doing it to protect the economic interests of school leadership to the detriment of everyone else.

Shawnee Mission, Olathe, and other school boards want to give the appearance of listening to the community, but they go to great lengths to stifle public comments that run counter to their political agenda.

Wichita school district stifles competition

Urban Preparatory Academy in Wichita is a private K–8 school that opened for the 2014–15 school year.[166] Its founder and headmaster, Rev. Wade Moore, opened the school to serve "low-income and mixed-income students . . . with a view to educating all students at the same high level, irrespective of socioeconomic, racial, ethnic or other status.[167]

He told the *Wichita Eagle* that the school would provide an education focused on business, entrepreneurship, and cultural awareness. He said cultural awareness is "more than a racial thing." Moore added, "We're creating a different kind of culture here—a culture of professionalism, a culture of respect, a culture of higher learning earlier."[168]

Moore is the pastor at Christian Faith Center, which purchased the vacant Mueller Elementary school building from the Wichita school district for $40,000 in 2013. Urban Prep originally was a K–5 school but eventually expanded to K–8 because of its popularity with parents and students. All students left the Wichita public school system; the vast majority attend Urban Prep tuition-free on scholarships awarded through the state's tax-credit scholarship program described earlier and other financial aid.

Students coming from the Wichita public schools are far behind where they should be academically. Moore talks about one student who came into the second grade at Urban Prep and scored a 1.8 on a reading test in September, meaning the child was reading at the level of a child with one year and eight months' capability. By May, the child scored a 3.7 on the reading test, gaining almost two years' worth of learning in a year and reading seven months *above* grade level.

Another student came to Urban Prep in the third grade scoring 1.2 on the math test (1.8 years below grade level). The student was considered learning disabled by the public school system but was placed in regular education at Urban Prep. By May, the student's score was 3.2, having gained two years' worth of learning and getting much closer to grade level. Moore says gains like these are more the rule than the exception.

He says they also see significant behavior improvement, especially in students' first year at Urban Prep after attending public school. He attributes the behavior and academic changes to students and parents having hope for a better future.

> Many students come here thinking no one cares about them at school. They know they are behind, and they are embarrassed by not being able to read and do math at grade level. And that's a big part of the behavior problems. But their behavior gets a lot better when they see how hard our staff works to get them caught up, and that gives students and their parents hope that they didn't believe was possible.
>
> One parent recently emailed me, saying, "I don't care if I have to work two or three jobs. My kids will attend Urban Prep."

Happy kids with better outcomes at Urban Prep did not sit well with the Wichita public school district. Officials viewed the situation through the single myopic lens of money, which is common throughout Kansas. In their view, Urban Prep costs them about $9,324 for each student who left for a better educational opportunity, which is hardly a drop in its budget bucket.[169] With enrollment at fifty students in 2017, the foregone revenue was less than 1% of the district's $574 million operating budget that year.[170]

Many state and local education officials act as though they "own" students and are entitled to every penny a student can generate. So with utter disregard for the educational interests of low-income students, the Wichita School Board took action in 2017 to ensure that its abandoned school buildings could never be used to compete with the district.

In May 2017, Wichita School Board members voted to sell another abandoned school, adding a clause to the contract prohibiting the buyer from operating it as a publicly funded school.[171] Board member Lynn Rogers, who later became Governor Laura Kelly's running mate as lieutenant governor and is now state treasurer, told the *Wichita Eagle*, "I don't think we want to use our tax dollars and basically help someone else start a school that would compete against us."[172]

The Wichita district notoriously produces dismal student outcomes, especially for low-income students. For example, the 2021 state assessment shows two-thirds of low-income sixth-graders below grade level, and only 12% are proficient. Preventing competition is tantamount to condemning students to a life of under-achievement, but education officials will not allow anything to interfere with what they perceive as their "right" to taxpayer money.

Urban Prep isn't the only victim of the Wichita School District's efforts to prevent competition.

The Phillips Fundamental Learning Center is a non-profit organization in Wichita that helps children who struggle to learn to read.[173] PFLC empowers children, especially those with dyslexia, by teaching them to read, write, and spell. It educates adults by providing research-based literacy programs, and helps parents better understand their children's educational and health needs. It has a teacher and parent education center and a private school for children with dyslexia.

According to the Yale Center for Dyslexia & Creativity, dyslexia "is an unexpected difficulty in reading for an individual with the intelligence to be a much better reader. It is most commonly due to a difficulty in phonological processing (the appreciation of the individual sounds of spoken language), which affects the ability of an individual to speak, read, spell and, often, learn a second language." Dyslexia affects 20% of the population and represents more than 80% of all those with learning disabilities.[174]

PFLC initially was located in the Parklane Shopping Center, but rapid enrollment increases prompted the board to search for a new location with room for expansion in 2015. Executive Director Jeanine Phillips and board member Roger Lowe led the search, during which they became aware that two developers were willing to donate a facility they were acquiring.

David Burke and Dave Wells were purchasing the former Wichita School District headquarters for an apartment development. They told Lowe and Phillips they would also buy a vacant school building from the Wichita district, Price Elementary, and deed Price to PFLC free and clear the day after they purchased it.[175]

Lowe says Burke and Wells filed a revised purchase offer with the district in January 2016 to purchase both properties. But the Wichita school district refused to sell them Price Elementary upon learning they planned to donate the building to PFLC.

Lowe says he and Phillips then met with Wichita Superintendent John Allison and offered to buy Price for $350,000, which was $10,000 more than the appraised value. But Lowe said the 259 Board again refused to sell the school to PFLC.

The district responded that they were undecided whether to keep Price for storage or what they would do with the facility. So, we proceeded to arrange for a showing of Emerson, another vacant school.

We made a presentation to the Wichita School Board to publicly request that they sell Price or Emerson to PFLC so they could accommodate more dyslexic kids. A mother of one of our students told the board that her child was enjoying and developing in PFLC's day school, but she was rudely interrupted. The board chair informed her that she had over-extended her five-minute limit. She was not permitted time to finish her important message about the success that her young child was enjoying. The chair then picked up a paper and said that the board would take a couple of years to study the best usage of the vacant buildings. A few months later, the Wichita School Board put Price on the market, but with a proviso that the building and land could not be used for a private school.[176]

Lowe says that throughout the time Price and Emerson sat vacant, the utilities were left on, and the buildings and the land were maintained, placing unnecessary costs on taxpayers.

He says the delay did not deter the PFLC board, "and in fact strengthened the resolve of the board, leading to a major campaign to include land purchase, building cost, scholarships for both students and teachers, operations, moving, etc., to strengthen the mission of FLC to help more children from all, walks of life. The campaign was appropriately titled "Transforming Education."

Lowe says they finally rented a vacant facility from the city and will continue renting until June 2023, when they move into their new building.

It's good that donors stepped up to transform education at PFLC, because the Wichita school district certainly hasn't. The 2021 state assessment shows that 51% of Wichita third-grade students read below grade level, and only 21% are proficient. Reading ability is even worse in high school, with 53% below grade level and just 14% proficient.[177]

Pournelle's Iron Law of Bureaucracy

Jerry Pournell was a scientist who specialized in operations research and human factors research.[178] He couched his research findings as "laws," including one he called "Pournelle's Iron Law of Bureaucracy." Pournelle said there will always be two kinds of people in any bureaucratic organization:

First, there will be those who are devoted to the goals of the organization. Examples are dedicated classroom teachers in an educational bureaucracy, many of the engineers and launch technicians and scientists at NASA, even some agricultural scientists, and advisors in the former Soviet Union collective farming administration.

Secondly, there will be those dedicated to the organization itself. Examples are many of the administrators in the education system, many professors of education, many teachers union officials, much of the NASA headquarters staff, etc. [179]

According to Pournelle, the Iron Law states that the second group will gain and keep control of the organization in every case. It will write the rules and control promotions within the organization.

David Dorsey says Pournelle's Iron Law of Bureaucracy was prevalent throughout his teaching career. "I think what the school boards and administrators are doing in terms of student outcomes is secondary to their own needs and wants as bureaucrats. So they're going to do what's best for them and whatever happens to the students happens. There may be specific students that they're trying to improve, but I think overall the approach is not geared to improve student outcomes."[180]

Dorsey believes some teachers and principals share his concern but don't speak up because the system strongly discourages everything it perceives as dissent.

"I worked with a lot of teachers who were just shaking their heads and saying, 'This isn't what I signed up for.' There's a lot of out-of-classroom stuff that they're required to do, and principals are kind of the same way. They were less likely to speak up because they were kind of comfortable with their positions as principals—a 'don't rock the boat' kind of thing."

He says substantive improvement cannot occur without the legislature getting involved.

If you . . . follow the bureaucracy, and if you go back to the Iron Law, you see that [the bureaucracy] sees that [its] needs are met first. So unless somebody says, 'Hey, we're going to change the way we do this, and we're going to force you to change,' that's not going to happen. The constant refrain is, 'We'd be doing better if we just had more money. And then, when things don't get better, it's, 'Well, that's not enough money. We just need more money.'

So I think the legislature has to get involved, and I really think the best way to do it is to open up the channel for . . . education choice. You get some competition in there, rattle some cages and get people, especially school administrators, to go, 'Hey, if we don't do this, then students have an option of going somewhere else.' So I think [that] that is going to be about the only way it happens. If you're looking for them to look inwardly in a sort of self-reflection and say, 'Hey, we need to do a better job,' that's just not going to happen.[181]

Former state board of education member Kathy Martin agrees that the legislature must get more involved.

I think the legislature needs to really provide oversight and let the school district know that they're providing oversight. I think that sometimes the school administration and the different organizations they belong to are controlled, not by serving the best interest of the kids, but by overlooking the kids and just thinking about what's good for the district, what financial things look good for the district. For years, our administrators—outside of the principals especially—have had some pretty terrific salaries. So it's kind of tough to say that they're doing the right thing sometimes without a lot of oversight. It can be really tough when people think power and money are what should be driving the education system, and that's not what we need here in our schools.[182]

Change the constitution to give kids a fighting chance
The fact that no individual, like a governor, can be held accountable for the performance and actions of the public education system only encourages the kind of behaviors recounted throughout this book.

The elected state board of education could press school districts to resolve race-based and income-based educational discrimination by withholding accreditation, but there is no hope of that happening.

Some state school board members might be willing to take student-focused positions and challenge the department of education and school districts if that was the position of the majority of the ten-member board. But if so, their desire to be re-elected—for whatever reason—is taking priority, and that relegates doing what is best for students to be a preference, but not a principle.

Massachusetts has a Model One education governance system—the governor appoints the majority or all members of the state board of education, which selects the state superintendent of schools. Under Massachusetts law, the state superintendent has the authority to take over poorly performing schools, and *The Wall Street Journal* reports that that is about to happen.

> In September, Matt Hills, a member of the state Education Board, pricked some consciences by saying he was starting to feel "complicit" for not raising the possibility of receivership—a state takeover. Jeffrey Riley, the state education commissioner, then ordered a formal assessment of [Boston Public Schools]—a prerequisite for receivership. Teams of observers have sat in on classes and talked to teachers, students, and staff.[183]

The Boston school system is "steaming with fervor for social justice," but the district "still does a poor job of educating kids, especially the majority who are Hispanic and Black. According to the article, only 25% of Black elementary students test at grade level in English.

In Kansas, only 10% of Black students are proficient in English language arts across all grade levels in the Wichita, Kansas City, and Topeka School Districts. Yet each district is fully accredited and under no pressure to improve without any one individual who is accountable to voters.

Article 6 of the Kansas Constitution should be amended to have the governor appoint state school board members to serve in advisory roles. The department of education should be a cabinet agency under the governor's supervision, just like every other executive branch agency. And the legislature should have no less authority over the public education system than it does over any other government agency.

Kansans must also amend the constitutional language regarding school funding to restore its original intent.

The Kansas Supreme Court in *U.S.D. No. 229 v. State* (1994) wrote, "[T]he issue is whether SDFQPA [School District Finance and Quality Performance Act] satisfies the constitution by providing suitable financing, not whether the level of finance is optimal or the best policy."[184]

Kansas State Constitution Art. 6, §6(b) says, "The legislature shall make suitable provision for finance of the educational interests of the state. No tuition shall be charged for attendance at any public school to pupils required by law to attend such school, except such fees or supplemental charges as may be authorized by law."[185]

The court's 1994 opinion established legal precedent that the constitutional meaning of "shall make suitable provision" compels the legislature to create a system of finance, such as a formula for funding schools. Indeed, the second sentence of KS Const. Art. 6, §6(b) effectively says, "but don't make tuition part of the formula."

But the 2005 Kansas Supreme Court ignored legal precedent and declared that the courts could indeed tell the legislature how much to spend on public education. According to KPI legal scholar Caleb Stegall, who is now a justice of the Kansas Supreme Court, the court arguably violated the Separation of Powers doctrine with its funding order.[186]

> The legislative power of the purse is inviolate. James Madison wrote that "the House of Representatives cannot only refuse, but they alone can propose, the supplies requisite for the support of government. They, in a word, hold the purse." Madison extolled the power of the purse in Britain as the one mechanism whereby "an infant and humble representation of the people gradually enlarging the sphere of its activity and importance, and finally reducing, as far as it seems to have wished, all the overgrown prerogatives of the other branches of the government." He concluded that "this power over the purse may, in fact, be regarded as the most complete and effectual weapon with which any constitution can arm the immediate rep-resentatives of the people, for obtaining a redress of every grievance,

and for carrying into effect every just and salutary measure." Should the Legislature give up the power of the purse, or allow it to be invaded by another branch of government, the people lose their most effective way to limit "the overgrown prerogatives of the other branches of the government."

Hamilton wrote that while the '[l]egislature . . . commands the purse,' the "judiciary, on the contrary, has no influence over either the sword or the purse; no direction either of the strength or of the wealth of the society; and can take no active resolution whatever."

This founding principle was enshrined at Kansas's founding as well. The state constitution expressly vests the authority of the purse in the Legislature, and makes it clear that taxation and appropriation are exclusively legislative powers.[187]

A little over a decade later, the Kansas Supreme Court, in another "Here, hold my beer" demonstration, compelled the legislature to further increase funding by more than $1 billion in *Gannon v. State of Kansas*.

Knowing they can count on the progressive activist Kansas Supreme Court to keep the money flowing without an ounce of accountability, education officials are incentivized to continue doing as they wish. The court bizarrely cited low achievement as "evidence" that schools are underfunded in awarding the $1 billion increase. But school attorneys wanted more than $2 billion, so it's only a matter of time until they return to court and ask for the other billion. Indeed, the court ruling creates a perverse incentive *not* to improve achievement.

Changing a state constitution is a huge lift. It requires a two-thirds vote of the house and the senate, and the education lobby will mount an epic fight to preserve the status quo without regard to the damage done to students. Winning the battle to revise Article 6 will, therefore, likely take multiple legislative sessions, and in the meanwhile, the legislature can implement statutory reforms to give kids a fighting chance.

Chapter 6—Choice, Transparency, and Accountability Give Kids a Fighting Chance in Florida

Florida was one of the worst states in the nation for student achievement in 1998. Only 12% of low-income students in the fourth grade could read proficiently, and just 11% in the eighth grade. Students who were not low-income were also doing poorly, with only 31% reading proficiently in both grades.

But in 2019, Florida was ranked #3 on the National Assessment of Educational Progress (NAEP), using an eight-score composite (reading and math, low-income and not low-income, fourth grade and eighth grade).[188] Low-income students are ranked #1 in fourth-grade reading and math, as are Hispanic students. Black students are ranked #5 in fourth-grade reading and #4 in fourth-grade math.

How did Florida bring about this remarkable transformation? Can states like Kansas replicate Florida's success?

The answers are in a thirty-five-minute documentary called *Giving Kids a Fighting Chance*. Kansas Policy Institute interviewed former Governor Jeb Bush and education officials on the twentieth anniversary of the revolution so parents and legislators across the nation can learn and be inspired by their efforts.

Bush explains what he and his team inherited:

So in 1998, I ran for governor saying that we needed to change our public education system. And I laid out a plan to do so in 1999. I got a chance to work with the Florida Legislature to implement probably the most meaningful suite of reforms up till that . . . the country had seen.

We graded schools A through F. We gave School Recognition dollars out for schools that showed improvement. We gave vouchers out for schools that were failing. And the net effect of all this was a turbulent time, certainly, but we turned the system upside down. And it was based on literally as a candidate going to visit 250 schools in a way that put a human context around this.

I never forget going to Seminole High School, where a kid was preparing to take the high school graduation tests and required an eighth-grade level aptitude. And he couldn't answer a question, which was "A baseball game started at 3:00 and ended at 4:30. How long was the game?"

If you have enough of those examples, just imagine what his world would look like going forward where we had these incredibly low expectations, no consequence between excellence and failure, no consequence between mediocrity and improvement. And it just kind of fueled me to be bigger and bolder, and the legislature went along with it, which I'm very grateful for.

And that started us on a journey of perpetual reform in the state of Florida. It was clear to me that the future for children as adults would be dramatically better if we assured that they had a chance to learn, learn how to read, and to be able to acquire knowledge. Today, it is even a bigger deal. The net effect of this was we have rising student achievement in Florida that is the envy of many places in the country. [189]

Bush and his team took an "all of the above" approach. The feeling was that students didn't have time to wait for the adults in the system to try one reform at a time. Their "secret sauce" combines choice, transparency, account-ability measures, and a heavy dose of courage to withstand opposition.

School choice in Florida

According to EdChoice (formerly the Friedman Foundation for Educational Choice), Florida offers K–12 students and their families several types of school choice, including five private school choice programs, charter schools, magnet schools, homeschooling, and inter- and intra-district public school choice via open enrollment policies.[190]

The Family Empowerment Scholarship Voucher Program allows public school students from low- and middle-income families to receive vouchers worth more than $7,000 to attend private schools. There were 74,418 students participating in fall 2020.

The Hope Scholarship Program provides scholarships worth up to $7,300 to victims of bullying and violence in public schools. Students may transfer to another public school district or a private school. The program served 189 students in fall 2021.

The Family Empowerment Scholarship ESA Program provides education savings accounts to students with special needs. Parents may use the funds to pay for various educational services, including private school tuition, tutoring, online education, home education, curriculum, therapy, postsecondary educational institutions in Florida, and other defined educational services. During the 2020–21 school year, 18,585 students participated with an average account value of more than $10,000.

Florida's Tax Credit Scholarship Program provided 85,030 low-income students and children in foster care an average scholarship of $6,684 to attend a private school.

The John M. McKay Scholarships for Students with Disabilities Program allows public school students with special needs who have Individualized Education Plans (IEPs) or 504 plans to receive vouchers to attend private schools or other public schools. During the 2021–22 school year, 26,451 students received scholarships averaging $9,631.

This robust menu of choice options benefits all students in Florida. The options break the public schools' monopoly and force the schools to compete. T. Willard Fair, president and CEO of the Urban League of Greater Miami, explains it well:

> It does extend to the individual student; then it extends to the individual school. Then it extends to all of the other schools. And then all the other students began to say, wow, what's going on over there? If I can go down the street and get this kind of return, if I don't want everybody to go down the street, I better figure out how to give equal return where I am.[191]

Former lieutenant governor, senate president, and teacher Toni Jennings also speaks to the benefits of competition:

The more competition we had in education, the better off we be-came. So I for one believe that competition is good. But you will hear those who say, "Oh no, you're making the public schools compete with others." Well, those children are going to have to go out and compete with others in the workaday world.[192]

Education officials in Kansas have vigorously opposed all forms of school choice in Kansas. Their laundry list of objections is long and is discussed in greater detail later in Chapter 6. Suffice it to say that every one of their objections has at least one of these charac-teristics in common:

- They are system-focused, not student-focused;
- They are based on speculation and myth, not fact; and of course,
- Money, money, money.

The education lobby tries to abolish the state's only choice pro-gram almost every year—the tax credit scholarship for low-income students. Kansas technically allows charter schools, but the law is structured to prevent competition. Charters in Kansas must be ap-proved and supervised by a public school district. That's like Sam's Club having to get permission from Costco to open a store, and it has the desired effect. There are only nine charter schools in Kansas, and most of the enrollment is in two that are virtual schools.[193]

Kansas came within one vote of expanding competition in 2021. An education savings account measure for low-income students and those with disabilities passed the house, but it died in the senate on a 20–20 tie. However, a different school choice program—Open Enrollment—passed in the 2022 session as part of Senate Substitute for House Bill 2567.[194] The legislation creates a transfer system for nonresident students between school districts based on the student capacity of each unified school district. Students had been able to transfer outside their home district if approved by the receiving district. The new legislation mandates approval if the receiving district has capacity.

But even this innocuous measure of competition was vigorously opposed by the education bureaucracy.

The usual suspects offered a variety of objections in committee testimony, with most focusing on inconveniences to the receiving districts. However, two school districts stood out, effectively saying open enrollment would force them to accept students they don't want—kids from low-income families or who have special needs.

Olathe Superintendent Brent Yeager and Blue Valley Superintendent Tonya Merrigan issued a rather elitist joint statement that belies their professed devotion to diversity and inclusion: "[W]e are certain to get a rush of special education students . . . as we already get inquiries almost daily from non-resident parents trying to enroll as both of our districts have a reputation of offering superior special education services."[195]

The districts noted that housing costs in wealthy areas contribute to high student achievement.

> While we can certainly empathize with parents in lower-performing districts, both Blue Valley and Olathe are among the highest-performing districts in Kansas—indeed competing nationally—and, as such, would find our districts overwhelmed with requests from non-residents. Without intending to sound elitist, it is nonetheless true that housing costs in our districts often provide a check on resident student growth now.[196]

Claiming that Olathe and Blue Valley are high-performing districts is highly deceptive. Blue Valley, and to a lesser extent, Olathe, have better outcomes than other districts in Kansas. Still, it is more a matter of not being as low as those districts rather than being "high-performing." The 2021 state assessment shows a quarter of Blue Valley high school students below grade level in math and less than half on track for college and career. Olathe is worse, with 38% below grade level and only a quarter on track.

In another slap at poor people, Blue Valley and Olathe say it isn't fair for their well-off residents to pay to educate kids from the other side of the tracks.

What we believe our local districts' taxpayers would find particularly egregious is that their *taxes would be paying for non-resident students* (emphasis in original), meaning the local resources for our resident students would be spread even further. While we would receive state BASE aid for these students, the same is not true for capital outlay, bond and interest, and other weightings based on property valuations.[197]

Merrigan and Yeager know that local taxpayers only provide a portion of total funding. State aid—money from taxpayers across Kansas—accounts for 49% of Blue Valley's budget and 64% in Olathe.[198] Low-income families in all parts of Kansas contribute a portion of the state aid that Blue Valley and Olathe collect, but Merrigan and Yeager don't want to acknowledge that.

Rep. Kristey Williams told KSHB-TV that their argument doesn't hold water: "I don't understand the pushback on that. I think that just because I can't afford a home in a certain district, it doesn't mean I shouldn't have the advantages that that district provides their students, and there are differences."[199]

Williams's point is reinforced by research showing that artificial gerrymandered school district borders lead to racial segregation and lower achievement. An article by Emily Bramhall for Housing Matters discusses why segregation between school districts matters for educational equity.

Across the country, most public school students live in racially concentrated school districts where most White students live in predominantly White districts, and most Black students live in predominantly Black districts. School district boundaries fuel racial inequalities in access to educational opportunities by perpetuating the link between residential segregation and school segregation. These divisions shuffle some students into districts with well-resourced, opportunity-rich schools and others into districts with fewer resources, shaping the trajectory of students' lives.[200]

An Urban Institute study entitled "Dividing Lines" concludes, "[W]ith just small changes to these [attendance] boundaries, district officials could create more integrated schools and potentially increase opportunities for Black and Hispanic students."[201]

Boundaries in four Shawnee County, Kansas, school districts reinforce the conclusion of the Urban Institute study.

Table 16: Achievement and Economic Characteristics				
District	% Proficient in Math	Median HH Income	Median Home Price	Owner Occupancy Rate
Topeka	17%	$48,319	$ 91,400	54%
Auburn-Washburn	34%	$78,264	$ 194,300	73%
Seaman	32%	$76,987	$ 156,100	85%
Shawnee Heights	27%	$81,544	$ 162,100	90%

Source: KS Dept. of Education, censusreporter.org

Table 17: Enrollment				
District	% White	% Black	% Hispanic	% Other
Topeka	35.1%	17.5%	33.8%	13.9%
Auburn-Washburn	74.1%	4.4%	8.5%	13.2%
Seaman	80.6%	2.8%	9.2%	7.5%
Shawnee Heights	66.1%	6.0%	17.1%	10.9%

Source: Kansas Dept. of Education

Table 16 shows that Topeka has a much lower median household income, median home price, and owner-occupancy rate than the other three districts. Topeka also has a much lower math proficiency rate on the 2021 state assessment.

Table 17 shows enrollment by race/ethnicity for the same year. Topeka is the only minority-majority district, with 35% White students and 65% Black, Hispanic, and Other race/ethnicity, while the others are between 66% and 81% White.

David Dorsey prepared this analysis for Kansas Policy Institute, noting the historical paradox:

The irony that shouldn't be lost on this example is that it was the very city of Topeka that was the subject of the historic *Brown v. Board of Education* case that struck down the practice of racial segregation in the nation's public schools. That decision was over a half-century ago, but de facto segregation based on economic factors is alive and well. [202]

Mike O'Neal says the state's tax credit scholarship program for low-income students is a good start but not near enough.

This is the civil rights issue of our time. Yes, families who can afford choice have choice. Families that can't afford choice have no choice. Not even in the public school system. They are locked into a zip code, for God's sake. In what universe does it make any sense that the quality of a child's education depends on the zip code they live in? The school establishment fought us on open enrollment this year. You've got Johnson County schools that don't want to have anything to do with any students from Wyandotte because it will spoil their gene pool, I guess. And that has got to stop. And so, we are at least making efforts to not have the socio-economically challenged, the low-income students, behind when it comes to school choice.[203]

Fortunately, the Merrigan/Yeager brand of educational discrimination did not prevail, even though several legislators tried to scuttle the open enrollment legislation during the house and senate floor debates.[204]

Rep. Valdenia Winn said open enrollment would only benefit "those rich kids, those middle-class kids" whose parents can afford to transport them to another district. Rep. Jo Ella Hoye concurred, saying, "[I]t is going to only be available to families that can afford the gas, that can afford the vehicle to transport them to the . . . school that they're choosing. There is not going to be opportunity for families that don't have schedules that can afford them a commute that can afford them the time in the morning."

There are at least two serious problems with their contention. First, a literature review by Reason Foundation's Director of Education Reform, Aaron Garth Smith, finds contradictory evidence. He cites one study in Michigan (Cowen, Creed & Kessler, 2015) that found "Black, low-income, and lower-performing students are more likely than their peers to participate in open enrollment." However, the study finds they're also the most likely among participants to exit the program. [205]

Smith cites a California study that notes, "Participating students have varied demographic backgrounds, including about 27 percent low-income and 65 percent non-white. However, the share of participating low-income students is lower than the share for home school districts."[206]

Other studies cited by Smith did identify "opportunity gaps" for economically disadvantaged families, but some still participated. And that raises the other significant problem with the claim that low-income students won't proportionally participate in open enrollment.

Disallowing open enrollment means that no low-income students can participate and are forced to stay in some of the worst-performing schools in the state. Choice opponents offer no alternative to improve outcomes for the students who most need choice because their focus is on what's best for the system, not for students.

Rep. Jarrod Ousley said, "When a student transfers out of there, that base state aid will follow that student. That will be a hit financially to those districts that perhaps are already suffering."[207]

Who cares if students are leaving for a better educational opportunity that will prepare them to be successful in life? The financial interest of the system is what matters most to the bureaucracy and its supporters. Winn said open enrollment is a "zero-sum game because if they leave this school district, they go to another one. They leave here, the funds go with them."

Rep. Chuck Schmidt called open enrollment "a solution looking for a problem." Schmidt spent thirty-three years in education as a teacher, a principal, and he was the superintendent of the Mission Valley School District.[208] The 2021 state assessment results show that 43% of high school students in Mission Valley are below grade level in math, and only 3% are proficient. In what universe is that not a problem?

Several other legislators also attempted to deflect attention from dismal student achievement results. Senator Pat Pettey, another retired educator, said, "So when we talk about our how our children are performing, and when you hear about Level 1, Level 2, Level 3,

Level 4, and some people saying, 'Oh, they should be performing at Level 3 and Level 4, we're not. Our children are performing the majority of them at Level 1 and Level 2, and Level 2 is adequate.'"[209]

Remember, students performing in Level 1 are below grade level; those in Level 2 have a basic understanding of the material and are considered at grade level but still need some degree of remedial training to be proficient.

Pettey then doubled down on her misrepresentation of achievement, saying, "Every school district is providing a quality education." Some students get a quality education in Kansas, but many do not. For example, in Pettey's home district of Kansas City, Kansas, 71% of high school students are below grade level in math, and only 7% are proficient.[210]

Pettey also tried the "we have higher standards than most states" dodge to excuse poor performance. But as explained in Chapter 2, proficiency comparisons to other states on the NAEP test is unaffected by state standards. Only about a third of students read proficiently according to NAEP, and proficiency on the state assessment is only marginally better. That may be "adequate" for Senator Pettey, but it's not for many parents.

But the prize for the most absurd objection to open enrollment goes to state school board member Michelle Dombrosky. She told KMBC-TV, "This bill destroys representative government."[211] Her hard-to-follow logic goes like this: parents of nonresident students do not participate in school board or bond elections of the school district where their child attends, and that somehow moves toward the combining or dissolution of local school boards.[212]

That's nonsense, but irrational thoughts are ubiquitous when educrats are defending their turf.

Open enrollment is not the panacea for all that is wrong with student achievement, but it's another step in the right direction. It forces school districts to compete for students, which benefits all students. It wasn't easy for some legislators to vote for something opposed by the bureaucracy, and that's a good sign that parental demand for improvement is forcing change.

Transparency in student achievement

Every state must have an assessment test to monitor progress in student achievement. Most states report results in vague terms that do not give parents and legislators a clear understanding of how students are doing.

Kansas at one time used labels like Approaches Standard, Meets Standard, and Exceeds Standard.[213] But one cannot interpret results without knowing the definition of "standard." Now, Kansas reports results in Levels 1 through 4.[214]

Florida broke through the fog and used labels that everyone understands—A, B, C, D, and F.

According to the Florida Department of Education, a school's grade may include up to eleven components. There are four achievement components, four learning gains components, a middle school acceleration component, and components for graduation rate and college and career acceleration. Each is worth up to one hundred points in the overall calculation, and a formula determines the school grade based on the percentage of total points earned.[215]

Only 21% of schools received an A or a B, and 28% received a D or an F in 1999.[216] That transparency created pressure on schools to improve, and they responded. By 2002, about half received an A or a B, and only 11% were D/F schools. Florida raised the A–F standards in 2002 to make it more challenging to get high grades, and they did so eight more times by 2016. As of 2018, 58% are A/B schools, and only 7% are D/F schools.

ExcelinEd is a nonprofit organization founded by former Governor Jeb Bush that supports state leaders in transforming education to unlock opportunity and lifelong success for every child.

They say media and public attention from the A–F grading of schools prompts community support, and parents are more empowered to make better choices for their children.

> Transparency in evaluating schools attracts more attention—from extensive media coverage of individual school effectiveness to realtors who highlight good school grades as a selling point on the housing market. This attention brings more investments in time

and energy from families, teachers, administrators, policymakers, and all community leaders to support and improve schools.

Schools now have a real, tangible sign of their excellence and hard work. Despite any initial objections to school grades, it is not long before everyone begins displaying their grade on the school marquee, hanging banners, or doing local press about the fact that they earned the coveted A grade or jumped from a D to a B.

In an A–F system, low-performing schools are easily identified and communities rally around them. A–F states can share numerous stories of communities coming together to improve schools to raise student achievement.

For example, in one Florida district, an entire school board meeting was dedicated to how the district could become the first in the state with no C schools. That would not have happened if the old labels of "satisfactory," "making progress," and other vague language had still been in place. [217]

Fifteen other states followed Florida's lead with their own A–F grading systems. In order of adoption: Arizona, Indiana, Louisiana, New Mexico, Oklahoma, Utah, Alabama, Mississippi, North Carolina, Ohio, Arkansas, Georgia, Texas, Tennessee, and Michigan. [218]

Kansas does not have a state-sponsored A–F grading system, but as mentioned in Chapter 2, Kansas Policy Institute created one in 2017. It translates state assessment scores into letter grades based on the department of education's cut scores and definitions. [219]

A letter grade is assigned to each public and private school taking the state assessment based on a formula like a student report card, with equal weighting applied to individual letter grades to calculate a Grade Point Average. Each grade level tested by KSDE (grades 3–8 and 10) is assigned a grade for English language arts (ELA) and math for low-income kids and those who aren't low-income, so each grade tested earns four letter grades.

Table 18 shows the results from 2021 for grades three through eight and the tenth grade. Only one school out of 1,273 earned an A, and just 103 earned a B. That means only 8% of public schools are A/B schools, compared to 40% of private schools. On the flip side, 44% of public schools are D/F, but just 15% of the private schools are.

Table 18: A-F Grading - Grades 3-8 and 10				
Letter Grade	Public Schools		Private Schools	
	Number	% Total	Number	% Total
A	1	0%	1	1%
B	103	8%	48	39%
C	602	47%	55	45%
D	487	38%	17	14%
F	80	6%	1	1%
	1,273		122	

Table 19: A-F Grading - 10th Grade				
Letter Grade	Public Schools		Private Schools	
	Number	% Total	Number	% Total
A	0	0%	0	0%
B	5	1%	3	17%
C	86	24%	10	56%
D	219	62%	4	22%
F	44	12%	1	6%
	354		18	

Source: Kansas Dept. of Education 2021 state assessment, scores translated by Kansas Policy Institute.

The tenth-grade results in Table 19 tell an even more disturbing story, with 74% of public high schools being D/F schools versus 28% of private high schools. Kansas has no public high schools with an A and only five that earn a B.

Incentivize desired results
Bush says Florida also incentivizes the desired results with rewards for progress:

> The largest bonus program for teachers in the United States is the School Recognition dollars that exist in our accountability system. Every school that (gets) an A or shows improvement (a higher letter grade) gets $100 per student . . . wire transferred directly into the school. No cuts by the bureaucracy. And there are celebrations when schools have this kind of success. And 90% of that goes in the form of bonuses to teachers.[220]

He says the National Education Association—the primary teacher union—and their state affiliates oppose merit pay because "they want the power on top of their teachers. But teachers appreciate the fact that they're being rewarded for a job well done."

Bush is right. Rep. Kristey Williams, who chairs the Kansas House K–12 Budget Committee, introduced HB 2690 in the 2022 legislative session to create the Legislative Award for Excellence in Teaching Program. The legislation earmarked $50 million of state aid (less than 1% of total state aid) for teacher bonuses based on gains on the state assessment test and other measurable outcomes.[221]

Schools would be required to establish a teacher appraisal process to identify teachers deserving of merit-based bonuses. The teacher appraisal process would be exclusively based on teacher performance standards that evaluate whether the teacher: (1) exemplifies and promotes excellence in academic achievement through creative, consistent, and meaningful ways; (2) inspires and maintains high academic standards and expectations through thoughtful and relevant lessons and instruction; and (3) encourages and models attitudes and behaviors to promote academic success and well-being. The principal of an eligible school would oversee each teacher appraisal process and designate teachers who submit an application and deserve a merit-based bonus. Only the principal would have the authority to determine whether a teacher is deserving of a merit-based reward.

Predictably, the education bureaucracy opposed the legislation, claiming the sky would fall if a tiny portion of state funding were set aside for teacher merit pay.

The state board of education's testimony in opposition includes a mixture of condescension and hyperbole:

> While we are pleased that you are affirming that excellence in education provides students a path to success and thus the state certainly will also benefit, there are studies that do not support your claim that a student must first acquire academic success to acquire soft skills.[222] [There are academically successful individuals who reportedly have not mastered soft skills while, on the other hand, there are at least as many individuals who never acquired academic success but who have demonstrated they have the soft skills employers desire.] We

are also pleased you wish to be consistently informed of annual reviews of academic achievement on state assessments as well as interventions, goals and strategies that are being utilized to move all students toward academic gains. As you are aware, the department has annually presented this data to you and they will continue to do so.[223]

State board members seem more concerned about whether students have soft skills like being on time than whether they can read and do math at grade level. They absurdly imply that employers value soft skills more than academic competence, and as documented earlier, legislative presentations of student achievement consistently obscure the truth.

Their testimony also claims that in setting aside less than 1% of state funding for merit pay, "you are starving school districts of needed funds up front [*sic*] to accomplish these goals." School districts would not be "starved" by the merit pay program; they began the year with nearly $1 billion in operating cash reserves that primarily reflect funding left over from prior years.

The state board of education also objected to a request for additional data in the legislation, saying, "There is a limit to how much data the State Department of Education is realistically able to provide. They have limited staff and their main purpose is to provide the educators in the field with the data and training they need to make quality decisions and to provide any assistance districts may need in curriculum, etc."[224]

In other words, once again, it's, "Shut up, go away, we know what we're doing."

Opposition from the Kansas Association of School Boards (KASB) covered much of the same ground but without condescension, concluding, "KASB believes this bill will not actually accomplish its stated goals and will have the most negative impact on the highest need students that the bill is purportedly designed to assist."[225]

The Kansas PTA, which almost always sides with the bureaucracy, objected to the legislature sticking its nose in the bureaucracy's business. They called merit pay a "corporate tool" that is "not-replicable, ineffective, and potentially harmful when considered for a nonprofit, public education model." And, of course, the PTA objects to money being allocated for merit pay.[226]

Written testimony from the Kansas chapter of the National Education Association (KNEA) objected to not being consulted on the merit pay proposal. KNEA says the single salary schedule, which pays teachers based primarily on how they have been teaching without regard to effectiveness, "is the most transparent and equitable system."[227]

Third-grade reading initiative

The third grade is a critical time in a student's life. That is when they transition from learning how to read to using reading to learn. According to the Annie E. Casey Foundation report, children who are not reading proficiently by the end of third grade are four times more likely to drop out or fail to graduate from high school. For poor Black and Hispanic students, that likelihood doubles.[228]

So about twenty years ago, Florida passed a law that required every student to demonstrate a level of mastery and foundational reading skills before going on to fourth grade.

Former Governor Bush says there was also an investment by the state and the feds in helping teachers understand those practices and how to put them into action in their classrooms: "And I think the policy coupled with that investment in relearning was so important. That change in policy challenged our beliefs and assumptions. If we just pass kids along or hope they get better over time, they don't."[229]

The policy change is paying off. Figure 11 shows Florida trailed the nation in fourth-grade reading proficiency in 1998, with only 22% of students reading proficiently compared to the 29% national average.

Most recently, Florida was at 38% proficient, but the national average was lower, at 35%.

A similar effort was attempted in Kansas. The Senate Education Committee held a hearing on Senate Bill 169 in the 2013 legislative session, modeled after the Florida initiative. It was opposed by the Kansas Association of School Boards, Kansas National Education Association, and school district officials from Kansas City, Topeka, and Newton.[230]

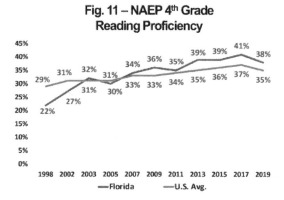

Fig. 11 – NAEP 4ᵗʰ Grade Reading Proficiency

Their primary objection was that kids would feel bad if they were held back. However, the real issue was that parents would be shocked to see how many third graders were below grade level, reflecting poorly on the adults in the system. Unfortunately, the legislation didn't go anywhere because Democrats and many Republicans were unwilling to upset the education bureaucracy, and there was a lack of support among house and senate leadership.

The Kansas State Legislature finally passed a version of the third-grade reading initiative in April 2022. The Every Child Can Read Act is included in Senate Substitute for House Bill 2597.[231] According to the Conference Committee Report Brief, the legislation requires each school district to provide opportunities for students to participate in targeted educational interventions. Literacy must be attained through the Science of Reading, evidence-based reading instruction, and necessary competencies to achieve proficiency. Schools are also required to follow and use the framework of KSDE's Dyslexia Handbook and ensure that competencies are achieved through literacy instruction in phonics, vocabulary development, reading fluency, and reading comprehension.

It is stunning that something as essential as a literacy program must be ordered by a state legislature, but that is symbolic of a public education system that de-emphasizes academics and is devoid of accountability.

It takes courage to stand up for students against bureaucratic opposition
The fourth ingredient in Florida's recipe for success—courage—is essential because the education establishment resists change. And there was a lot of resistance in Florida, as Bush explains: "So over time, we did have one statewide newspaper, large newspaper, be supportive in Jacksonville, but generally people were opposed to this, to begin with in the press. The teachers union was opposed to it. The school boards were opposed to it. The blob, if you will."[232]

Toni Jennings, a former teacher and former lieutenant governor of Florida, says some of the pushback ironically underscored the need for reform.

"You had opposition from the teachers union. You had opposition from time to time from parents. It was amazing. I can't tell you the number of letters we got written by schoolchildren. It was obvious they wrote them in class. And the worst part of it was, I wanted to correct their grammar and their spelling and write back to their teacher and say, 'Is this what you're teaching?'"[233]

The opposition in Florida and Kansas is not about students. It's really about the adults in the system, as Bush notes:

> The issue of education is very political because in many school districts, many cities, many towns . . . the school districts were the largest employers. And so, the focus inevitably gets to the economic interests of the adults. We had dramatic reform, and the adults had done pretty (well). The idea that somehow you're going to destroy public education by embracing choice or accountability has just not been proven in Florida.[234]

Those who oppose choice, transparency, and accountability make dire predictions of what will happen or what might occur . . . because they cannot say "This is what **did** happen" in Florida or other states.

When presented with objections to one of those "might happen" scenarios, the best response is to respectfully ask for documentation like this: "I understand your concern, but educational choice has been around for more than twenty-five years. Can you show me evidence that (this) has occurred in states with robust choice options?"

The person objecting may only be repeating what they have been told because the education bureaucracy is adept at spreading scare tactics even when they know better.

"Choice will defund public schools" is one of the most common myths used to oppose change, and it's also one of the easiest to debunk. Per-student spending in Florida and Arizona, other states with robust choice options, is increasing faster than inflation. According to Dr. Ben Scafidi, inflation-adjusted current expenditures per student in Florida increased by 13% between 2000 and 2018.[235]

Education officials know, or at least should know, that a student leaving the district does not cause a decline in funding per student. The effect on school districts' finances is no different than when a student's family moves out of state.

Here's another myth: private schools aren't accountable like public schools. That claim is precisely backward . . . private schools *have* accountability, but public schools *do not*. Parents can vote with their feet if they are not satisfied with a private school; they can move their child to another private school or a public school. But nothing happens if public schools don't perform.

Dr. Michael McShane explains in "The Accountability Myth":

First, traditional public schools are not *financially accountable*. School spending is opaque. It is very difficult to determine just how much a school spends on the students that it educates. Schools, districts, and states have put up myriad barriers between taxpayers and schoolhouses. There is not uniform agreement as to what spending categories should "count" when it comes to calculating per-pupil expenditures, and the same district will publish multiple numbers in different outlets. If we don't know how or how much money is being spent, we cannot hold the people spending it accountable.

Second, schools are not *democratically accountable*. School boards are often held up as paragons of local democracy—close to the people, made up of non-professional politicians drawn from the body politic out of genuine interest for children, existing outside of the degradations of partisan politics. Oh, were that so. Unfortunately, school board elections are low-turnout affairs often conducted "off-cycle" to ensure low participation. They do not represent the views of the populace because only a tiny minority of the community participate in their election. What they do represent are the views of motivated and resourced interest groups, who are able to swing small elections in their favor.

Third, schools are not *educationally accountable*. Traditional public school advocates hold up the extensive testing and data-gathering systems that states operate and the ostensible consequences linked to those systems as evidence that public schools are held accountable for the education they provide. Even a cursory peek under the hood of these systems shows that they are so byzantine and manipulable that few, if any, schools ever actually meet with serious consequences for their poor performance.[236]

Another favorite myth pushed by opponents is that choice is really about dismantling public education. A few people on the fringe may not believe in government schools, but educational choice helps improve public education. Choice proponents don't want to abolish public education; they want to make it work for all students.

And it does, as shown in "Who's Afraid of School Choice" by Jason Bedrick:

From 2003 to 2020, Florida's gains on the National Assessment of Educational Progress (NAEP) have significantly outpaced the national average, increasing by 12.2 points and 6.7 points on 4th-grade Math and Reading, and 7.2 points and 6.1 points on 8th-grade Math and Reading. Likewise, a recent study of the competitive effects of school choice on district schools in Florida found "consistent evidence that as more students use scholarships to attend private schools, students in public schools most likely to experience heightened competition due to the program see positive effects" on Math and Reading scores.

Florida is not unique. Researchers at the University of Arkansas found a "strong and statistically significant association" between educational freedom (including the robustness of a state's school choice policies) and "both academic scores and academic gains." Indeed, 25 out of 28 empirical studies on the effects of voucher or tax-credit scholarship programs on the academic performance of students who remain at their traditional public schools find statistically significant positive effects. One finds no visible effect, and two find a small negative effect.[237]

There are even some opponents who believe educational choice is about eliminating *private schools*. They fear that participation in a choice program puts private schools under government control. But that's not true.

Bedrick says private schools that take the money will not be controlled by government. Most school choice programs nationwide have a very light touch regarding regulations, including Kansas. The programs implemented and proposed in Kansas allow participating private schools to be accredited by many organizations other than the Kansas Department of Education. Also, any money going to private schools is under the direction of parents, not the department of education.

Accepting federal or state money does not obligate private schools to teach common core, critical race theory, social-emotional learning, or anything else, according to Bedrick. Private schools and Kansas public schools are not held to any curriculum standards even if they take state or federal money. Curriculum decisions in Kansas are made solely by local school boards or the individual private school. Local school boards can opt out any time they wish.

People who oppose choice, transparency, and accountability have all kinds of objections, but they will not directly answer this question: *"A third of Kansas students are below grade level in reading and math. So if none of these reforms are implemented, how many decades will it take the system to get all students to at least grade level?"*

Florida flourishes while Kansas goes backward
Florida's combination of choice, transparency, and accountability helped all students improve and directly attacked educational discrimination. Students of color and those from low-income families

are seeing the most significant gains, and their progress is dramatically above the national average.

In fourth-grade reading, Florida's low-income students jumped from 12% proficient to 28% between 1998 and 2019, while the national average improved from 13% to 21%. But results declined in Kansas. Table 20 shows a drop from 22% to 20%.

Table 20: 4th-Grade Low-Income Reading Proficiency			
State	1998	2019	% Change
Kansas	22	20	-9%
Arizona	10	18	80%
Florida	12	28	133%
National Avg.	13	21	62%
Table 21: 8th-Grade Low-Income Reading Proficiency			
State	1998	2019	% Change
Kansas	21	19	-10%
Arizona	12	16	33%
Florida	11	25	127%
National Avg.	14	20	43%
Source: National Assessment of Educational Progress			

Table 21 reflects a decline in eighth-grade proficiency from 21% to 19% for Kansas, while proficiency more than doubled in Florida, going from 11% to 25%.

Arizona, another state with robust choice options, also recorded significant gains for low-income students.

Tables 22 and 23 show that students of color also made remarkable progress relative to Kansas and the national average.

Table 22: 4th-Grade Hispanic Reading Proficiency			
State	1998	2019	% Change
Kansas	22	21	-5%
Arizona	8	20	150%
Florida	19	34	79%
National Avg.	13	23	77%
Table 23: 4th-Grade Black Reading Proficiency			
State	1998	2019	% Change
Kansas	15	15	0%
Arizona	11	21	91%
Florida	8	23	188%
National Avg.	10	18	80%
Source: National Assessment of Educational Progress			

Hispanic fourth graders in Florida jumped from 19% proficient to 34%, and they went from 8% to 20% in Arizona. Florida's Black students improved from 8% to 23%, and in Arizona, they jumped from 11% to 21%. Meanwhile, in Kansas, proficiency for Hispanic students declined, and Black students had no gains.

Florida's national rankings are equally impressive. In fourth-grade reading, Hispanic and low-income students are ranked #1 among the fifty states, and Black students are #5. In eighth-grade, Hispanic students are #4, low-income kids are #5, and Black students are #10.

Overall, Florida is ranked #3 on the eight-score composite based on reading and math, fourth grade and eighth grade for low-income students and their more affluent peers.[238] Kansas is ranked #27.

Here again, we see that money is not the driving force. Adjusted for the cost of living, 2019 total spending per student in Florida was only $11,008. It was $16,661 in Kansas, and the national average was $15,669.[239]

Bush says there is now broad support for the reforms among educators. "And today, you see superintendents of these large school districts that are proud of the fact that Florida is leading the way in terms of rising student achievement, they're embracing it, most teachers embrace it. There has been a change in mindset that is pretty dramatic."[240]

Legislators and parents in Florida and other states unwilling to accept persistent educational discrimination are giving kids a fighting chance by openly advocating for choice, transparency, and accountability. And their courage is making a real difference for students.

Kansas students can have the same opportunities to be successful in life if enough parents, grandparents, and business leaders are willing to get in the game.

Chapter 7—The Choice Is Yours: Give Kids a Fighting Chance or Accept the Status Quo

Some students in the Kansas public school system do well, but every measure of student achievement shows that more students are *not* proficient than are. More than 300,000 of the state's 465,000 students are *not* proficient in reading and math, based on the 2021 state assessment.[241]

The department of education's "Kansans Can" initiative and its cousin, the school redesign project, are showing no progress in improving overall achievement. Education officials say they want equality in education, but their actions show otherwise; they won't even follow state law to address race-based and income-based educational discrimination.

Many state and local education leaders have a long history of intransigence that eliminates any hope that the system will resolve educational discrimination. Some educators, particularly teachers and principals who have quietly made their feelings known, are displeased with the status quo, but they fear leadership will retaliate if they speak out. And history indicates their concerns are valid.

It will take external leadership to give Kansas kids a fighting chance, which former Governor Bush makes clear:

> We didn't have huge support amongst Democrats, but we had enough support to validate the idea. We have support from the business community. We had support amongst good teachers . . . [who] weren't threatened by accountability. In fact, they embraced it and wanted to see it. We had support among parents that wanted more choices, particularly lower-income parents that are assigned schools . . . so we built a coalition that was helpful.
>
> But I'll be honest with you. If you don't have a political leader willing to take the political risk to advocate big things and then to implement it in an intellectually honest way, a faithful way, to the ideas that can yield a good result, you're not going to get the benefits of reform. You have to be all-in.[242]

Kansas has never had a governor who champions choice, transparency, and accountability on behalf of students. Toward the end of his term in office, Republican Governor Sam Brownback (2011–18) called on the legislature to pass school choice measures and grade schools A–F in his 2017 State of the State address, but that was too little and too late.[243] He knew that achievement was dismally low upon taking office, as he privately acknowledged on several occasions. But Brownback was unwilling to take on the political fight with the education lobby.

The state's current governor, Democrat Laura Kelly, openly sides with the education establishment that effectively endorses race-based and income-based educational discrimination. Like all politicians, she says she is a big supporter of students, but her actions paint a different picture. She campaigned in 2018 on being the education governor, but her website shows her focus to be almost exclusively on money for the system.[244] The Kansas Schools page of her 2018 campaign website says nothing about achievement levels or educational discrimination, let alone efforts needed to tackle the problems.

House and senate members who voted for an education savings account bill in 2021 were disappointed that the measure failed by one vote in the senate, but they knew Kelly would have vetoed the bill had it passed.

Those 2021 votes in the house and senate represent the legislature's general division on significant education issues, falling into four camps—strongly support, somewhat support, somewhat opposed, and "over my dead body" opposed.

Those who are strongly supportive embody something German philosopher Arthur Schopenhauer once said: "All truth passes through three stages. First, it is ridiculed. Second, it is violently opposed. Third, it is accepted as being self-evident."[245]

A small group of house and senate members is not afraid to tell the truth about student achievement. They fearlessly faced ridicule and opposition in support of better educational opportunities for students.

The second tier includes somewhat supportive legislators who are more subtle in their actions. They will often vote for legislation but are hesitant to take the heat for being out in front.

Those in the "somewhat opposed" camp are split among two sub-groups. The first one includes Democrats who are secretly supportive but know their party will punish them if they vote their conscience, as in, another Democrat will primary them. This faction of "somewhat opposed" also includes some Republicans beholden to the education bureaucracy that helped elect them. The second sub-group has members who are opposed but are willing to have a civil discussion of issues.

The bi-partisan "over my dead body" group is all-in for the bureaucracy. These legislators are fully aware of the dismal state of student achievement, but their allegiance is to the system not the students.

Non-legislators generally fall into the same groups but with a few nuances.

Legislators know the sad state of student achievement, but that is not the case with many people outside the legislature and the education system. It is not uncommon for people to move up a tier from "somewhat support" and "somewhat opposed" once they understand student achievement facts and how the system works.

After a few years on the Wichita School Board, Joy Eakins transitioned from "strongly opposed" to "strongly support." Eakins explained her change of heart when she testified in support of education savings account legislation in 2021:

> Last Wednesday, I spoke at the hearing on remote/hybrid education and discussed how the design of the [COVID] School Gating Criteria prioritizes adult health over children's by painting a picture for boards about the community toll without considering the toll on children. I have included that article here with all relevant references to the data included in that report. I'm happy to answer any questions you may have had after having time to look at that data.
>
> When we find ourselves under intense pressure, that is when we find out what is really going on inside—where we have strengths and where we show weakness. The same is true for systems. This last year our systems have been under an inordinate amount of stress. And in the process, we have

seen that some school districts are built on what is right for kids and their families—while other districts have a different list of priorities. Yes—there are caring adults inside all those systems. There are even caring adults who lead some of those systems. But their voices are often muted, or they are afraid to speak up. The new voices you hear speaking up are those who are now seeing it.

When I ran for USD 259 [Wichita School Board] in 2013, I staunchly opposed measures like this bill. I believed that we could bring change from the inside and fix these issues for our most vulnerable students. So, what changed? Why am I here today? I got a good look at the inside of the system and saw what many of you see.

In the four and a half years I sat on the board, we had one meeting where student achievement data was brought for a discussion. The district reported that the results were encouraging—until I pointed out in the meeting that in five of our high schools, one of every two students was below grade level in Math. That was the last time we discussed state test results in a meeting.

Instead, the board talked about the new school facilities we should build, how to maximize the mill levy authority on our citizens, lawsuits against the state for more money, and balancing the budget by cutting programs for at-risk High School students to save SEIU labor contracts. We did discuss education—usually we talked about the new teaching practices we would impose on our highly educated and committed teaching staff or lament the discipline crisis our teachers faced without actually taking steps to solve the problem.

This continues today. This year, the Wichita School Board has taken public comments once—when required by law—but the teachers union and SEIU (Service Employees International Union) have spoken at every meeting. The board voted to lock parents out of watching their children participate in activities, even "safe" activities like cross country—and after that vote, one board member wondered if he would be allowed a pass to these same high school events. His child is in kindergarten.[246]

Here are two examples of what Eakins observed: According to the *Wichita Eagle*, in 2017, Wichita School Board member Betty Arnold declared that parents on district advisory panels shouldn't be allowed to speak at those meetings.

> In an e-mail to Eakins in March 2016, Arnold directed Eakins to tell two women who had been invited to participate in a student wellness committee that "the only role they can serve would be as observers."
>
> "Their attendance does not offer any special privileges such as actively being a part of the discussion and/or direction," Arnold wrote in the email, which Eakins shared with *The Eagle*. "Meetings are open but input from anyone other than committee members is not permitted."[247]

When Arnold served as board president in 2012, she admonished parents who wanted to discuss some issues with the board: "This board meeting is held in public, but it is not for the public, or of the public."[248]

Arnold was elected to the state board of education in 2021.[249]

Intimidation of this nature is becoming much more common, and it is essential to keep that in mind when discussing education issues with friends and associates. Many school employees are inundated with false information about achievement, school spending, and other subjects, so they will repeat the bureaucracy's talking points in the community. Teachers and others are told that their jobs are at risk because of "anti-public-education" efforts pushed by proponents of change. Combined with a healthy dose of intimidation, people come to believe what they've been told.

David Dorsey shares two experiences from his time as a public school teacher in Kansas that describe the abuse and indoctrination imposed on teachers:

> It's common practice at school staff meetings when principals dispense "bad news" to the staff that it is blamed on either "the state," but more commonly, the Republicans in the legislature. At one meeting when I was at Topeka, the principal told us the

problems would only go away if we voted out the Republicans. That was clearly over the line. I raised the issue with the superintendent, who chastised the principal. The principal [who didn't know it was me] called in the entire staff and yelled at us for squealing! In another example in Garnett, two reading teachers asked the superintendent for a few bucks to buy plastic bags. The request was just before an election, and the super told them—as they relayed it to me—that there would be no more money for materials if they kept voting for Republicans.[250]

The Overton Window: a model for understanding how ideas change
So how can you effect change in this kind of environment?

The late Joseph P. Overton developed a way of thinking about policy change in the mid-1990s that has helped move some pretty significant issues. Few people would have believed that Michigan, home of the United Auto Workers, would ever become a right-to-work state and eliminate mandatory union membership. It took time, but it happened in 2012, thanks in no small part to the Mackinac Center for Public Policy and The Overton Window.[251]

Overton was senior vice president at Mackinac when he died in 2003. He created The Overton Window of Political Possibilities to help understand how ideas in society change over time and influence politics.

The core concept is that politicians are limited in what policy ideas they can support—they generally only pursue policies that are widely accepted throughout society as legitimate policy options. These policies lie inside the Overton Window. Other policy ideas exist, but politicians risk losing popular support if they champion these ideas. These policies lie outside the Overton Window.

But the Overton Window can both shift and expand, either increasing or shrinking the number of ideas politicians can support without unduly risking their electoral support. Sometimes politicians can move the Overton Window themselves by courageously endorsing a policy lying outside the window, but this is rare. More often, the window moves based on a much more complex and dynamic phenomenon, one that is not easily controlled from on high: the slow evolution of societal values and norms.

Think for a minute about education policy. By and large, our society agrees that providing children with a formal education is a good thing. But how best to accomplish this policy is a wide-open question. There are dozens of different policies that could be used.

Now imagine the different policy options for providing children a formal education lined up along a spectrum. On one end, you'd find a policy idea to use the power of the federal government to provide education to all children—a top-down, centralized approach. On the other end of the spectrum, you'd find just the opposite policy idea: no government involvement whatsoever, leaving the provision of education to private citizens.

Virtually no politician endorses either one of the policies at the ends of this spectrum. We can posit then that these policies lie outside the Overton Window. The policies that politicians do champion—tax-funded public school districts, regulated private schools, independent public charter schools, etc.—exist between these two ends of the spectrum and are solidly within the Overton Window.

To get an idea of how the Overton Window can change over time, think about the Prohibition Era. Just a few generations ago, the sale and use of alcoholic beverages was made illegal by federal law, suggesting that this policy was safe inside the Overton Window. But fast forward to today when people poke fun of [sic] the folly of Prohibition and virtually no politician endorses making alcohol illegal again. The Overton Window has clearly shifted, and Prohibition is no longer within its borders.

The Overton Window doesn't describe everything about how politics works, but it does describe one key thing: Politicians will not support whatever policy they choose whenever they choose; rather, they will only espouse policies that they believe do not hurt their electoral chances. And the range of policy options available to a politician are shaped by ideas, social movements and shared norms and values within society.

All of this suggests that politicians are more followers than they are leaders — it's the rest of us who ultimately determine the types of policies they'll get behind. It also implies that our social institutions—families, workplaces, friends, media, churches, voluntary associations, think tanks, schools, charities, and many other phenomena that establish and reinforce societal norms—are more important to shaping our politics than we typically credit them for.[252]

The education bureaucracy wants concepts like choice, transparency, and accountability to be outside The Overton Window. If you want better educational opportunities, you have to move these subjects inside the window where they can be safely discussed.

You can do that with an invitation to a civil discussion.

Lead a discussion, not a lecture

Lecturing someone about the many reasons (you think) they are wrong is a sure-fire way to have an unproductive conversation. Even if someone is wrong, they must be allowed to walk away from previously held beliefs, and that takes a little planning.

As American philosopher Yogi Berra said, "You've got to be very careful if you don't know where you are going because you might not get there."[253]

It's possible to persuade someone to acknowledge they were wrong in one conversation, but they are likely to change their mind again when talking to someone with a different viewpoint. However, a consultative approach helps people reach their own conclusions, which are much harder to change.

Here are a few key tactics that help promote policy change:

- Ask questions.
- Show a little vulnerability.
- Help solve someone else's problem, not yours.
- Anticipate questions and objections, and get there first.

No one wants to buy something if they don't think they need it, which is also true with public policy issues. Gaining agreement that a problem exists is the first step.

A conversation with a friend might start with something like, "Have you seen the latest student achievement numbers? They are much different than I expected, based on what I have heard in the past."

An approach like this encourages engagement and grants permission to change one's mind. They weren't wrong; like you, they were given inaccurate information.

Next, share facts with emotional impact.

"According to the Kansas Department of Education, there are more high school students below grade level than are proficient and on track for college and career. That seems hard to believe, but it tracks with ACT results—only 21% of Kansas graduates are college-ready in English, reading, math, and science. Is that acceptable to you?"

Be prepared for the facts to be questioned. Some people may just be skeptical, or they might have a reason to discount the results, like questioning the reliability of standardized testing.

"I understand. But a recent state audit found that, even before the pandemic, about a third of Kansas graduates signed up for at least one remedial course in college. That seems like a pretty clear indication that many students are not getting the education they need in school.

"And what I find even more troubling is that it has been this way for a long time. How many more students will be left behind before something is done?"

If you believe achievement is unacceptably low and don't think that that will change very soon, you are faced with two options.

One option is to get involved. Share the stories in this book with your friends, neighbors, and business associates. Ask them how many more students must suffer race-based and income-based educational discrimination before they are willing to become part of the solution.

Rep. Kristey Williams says she does not see a pathway forward without the steady pressure of parents and legislators.

The other option is to do nothing, which is easy to justify. Everyone is busy . . . we elect people to solve these problems for us . . . it is a controversial topic, and you don't want to upset anyone . . . the list goes on. But adopting Option #2—doing nothing—effectively says you think that achievement is good enough (or at least not bad enough to warrant your engagement).

In *Giving Kids a Fighting Chance,* former governor Bush has a message for state and local elected officials who take the second option:

> If you're elected to an office, a state house or state senator or governor or any position of responsibility, what are you doing if you're not reforming the things to assure that the next generation has a fighting chance in this incredibly challenging and competitive world that we're moving towards?
>
> If you're not there to serve people and to change the things that are broken, what are you there for? Imagine what the world looks like a decade from now, twelve years from now, when a kindergartener is graduating from a school in Kansas that is capable of either getting a job [for which] they are career-ready or already having under their belt college-level work that makes it possible for them to graduate on time for a four-year degree. Their dreams are going to be broad and big. They're not going to be brought in big if we dumbed everything down and have what my brother called the soft bigotry of low expectations.
>
> This is the civil rights issue of our time, it's the economic issue of our times, and it is the social justice issue of our time. Political leaders need to get off the mat and start advocating more meaningful reforms so that there's rising student achievement so that dreams can come true.[254]

The choice is yours. What are you doing to give kids a fighting chance to succeed in life?

About the Authors

Dave Trabert is CEO of Kansas Policy Institute, where he also does research and writes on fiscal policy and education issues. He is the lead author of the tax policy book *What Was **Really** the Matter with the Kansas Tax Plan: The Undoing of a Good Idea.* His other published work includes "Removing Barriers to Better Public Education" and "Student-Focused Funding Solutions for Public Education."

He was an appointed member of the Kansas K–12 Student Achievement and Efficiency Commission. He currently serves on the Tax and Fiscal Policy Task Force and co-chairs the Education Finance Joint Working Group for the American Legislative Exchange Council.

The Wall Street Journal has published his commentaries, along with *National Review, Investor's Business Daily*, the *Washington Examiner*, TheHill.com, and other national publications. His work has also been published in many Kansas newspapers.

He graduated *cum laude* from West Liberty State College with a degree in business administration.

David Dorsey is a Senior Education Policy Fellow with Kansas Policy Institute. He does policy research on issues related to K–12 finance, student achievement, and education reform. Prior to joining KPI, Dorsey spent 20 years as a public school elementary teacher. He was both a classroom and specialty teacher and served in various leadership capacities in those schools.

Dorsey received a bachelor of science degree from the University of South Dakota with a major in political science and a minor in economics.

Appendix A—National Assessment of Educational Progress (NAEP) Proficiency in Reading and Math 2019

Appendix A - NAEP Proficiency								
	4th-Grade Reading		8th-Grade Reading		4th-Grade Math		8th-Grade Math	
State	Low-Income	Not Low-Income	Low-Income	Not Low-Income	Low-Income	Not Low-Income	Low-Income	Not Low-Income
U.S. Average	21%	51%	20%	46%	26%	58%	18%	48%
Alabama	16%	45%	14%	33%	16%	44%	9%	34%
Alaska	14%	37%	13%	33%	20%	47%	16%	41%
Arizona	18%	46%	16%	42%	22%	55%	21%	41%
Arkansas	24%	48%	21%	44%	24%	52%	17%	45%
California	20%	52%	18%	47%	19%	56%	16%	50%
Colorado	22%	54%	19%	49%	23%	61%	18%	49%
Connecticut	20%	57%	23%	52%	23%	63%	18%	52%
Delaware	17%	40%	16%	36%	23%	46%	13%	36%
Florida	28%	52%	25%	47%	38%	62%	19%	46%
Georgia	20%	56%	21%	50%	22%	63%	17%	53%
Hawaii	22%	44%	17%	38%	24%	53%	15%	37%
Idaho	26%	49%	25%	47%	31%	56%	22%	49%
Illinois	21%	50%	21%	50%	24%	54%	20%	46%
Indiana	24%	52%	25%	48%	33%	63%	23%	50%
Iowa	22%	46%	17%	43%	25%	57%	18%	44%
Kansas	20%	48%	19%	44%	25%	57%	20%	46%
Kentucky	25%	50%	23%	48%	29%	57%	18%	43%
Louisiana	18%	44%	19%	44%	20%	52%	14%	40%
Maine	23%	46%	24%	44%	27%	55%	19%	44%
Maryland	19%	51%	18%	48%	21%	56%	14%	46%
Massachusetts	26%	55%	24%	53%	28%	62%	25%	56%
Michigan	20%	45%	19%	43%	21%	52%	16%	43%
Minnesota	21%	49%	18%	43%	31%	66%	22%	56%
Mississippi	26%	54%	19%	45%	31%	67%	17%	46%

Appendix A - NAEP Proficiency (cont'd)							
	4th-Grade Reading		8th-Grade Reading		4th-Grade Math		8th-Grade Math	
State	Low-Income	Not Low-Income	Low-Income	Not Low-Income	Low-Income	Not Low-Income	Low-Income	Not Low-Income
Missouri	23%	51%	21%	45%	28%	56%	18%	45%
Montana	22%	49%	24%	42%	29%	55%	22%	45%
Nebraska	22%	50%	18%	45%	30%	60%	21%	48%
Nevada	24%	46%	20%	40%	25%	54%	16%	40%
New Hampshire	21%	47%	20%	45%	28%	55%	19%	47%
New Jersey	22%	56%	23%	54%	26%	64%	22%	57%
New Mexico	17%	48%	16%	43%	23%	51%	14%	40%
New York	20%	53%	22%	43%	24%	54%	21%	46%
North Carolina	21%	50%	20%	42%	26%	56%	20%	49%
North Dakota	22%	41%	19%	37%	27%	53%	20%	46%
Ohio	22%	53%	20%	53%	25%	59%	17%	54%
Oklahoma	20%	42%	17%	39%	24%	53%	16%	39%
Oregon	23%	52%	23%	47%	26%	57%	20%	46%
Pennsylvania	23%	55%	21%	46%	26%	65%	20%	53%
Rhode Island	21%	50%	18%	50%	26%	56%	12%	45%
South Carolina	20%	52%	19%	43%	23%	59%	16%	46%
South Dakota	23%	42%	17%	38%	25%	52%	22%	46%
Tennessee	18%	43%	17%	37%	22%	49%	15%	38%
Texas	19%	48%	15%	40%	32%	62%	19%	45%
Utah	22%	49%	25%	45%	32%	54%	19%	47%
Vermont	21%	47%	28%	47%	27%	47%	23%	46%
Virginia	20%	52%	18%	42%	30%	61%	19%	49%
Washington	22%	50%	21%	54%	24%	56%	23%	56%
West Virginia	22%	40%	19%	31%	19%	43%	15%	32%
Wisconsin	20%	48%	23%	50%	26%	59%	22%	54%
Wyoming	27%	49%	21%	41%	33%	56%	24%	44%

Source: National Assessent of Educational Progress

Appendix B—ACT College-Ready in English, Reading, Math, and Science

Appendix B - ACT College Readiness Kansas Graduates				
School Year	All Students	White Students	Hispanic Students	Black Students
2003	23%	25%	11%	5%
2004	24%	26%	11%	4%
2005	25%	27%	11%	4%
2006	25%	27%	11%	4%
2007	26%	28%	10%	6%
2008	26%	29%	11%	6%
2009	26%	29%	13%	5%
2010	28%	31%	12%	6%
2011	28%	32%	13%	6%
2012	29%	33%	13%	6%
2013	30%	35%	14%	7%
2014	31%	36%	14%	7%
2015	32%	37%	15%	8%
2016	31%	36%	15%	8%
2017	29%	35%	14%	6%
2018	29%	34%	13%	8%
2019	27%	32%	11%	7%
2020	23%	28%	11%	6%
2021	21%	25%	9%	5%
Source: ACT				

Appendix C—National Assessment of Educational Progress (NAEP) Productivity Index

2020 Spending and Achievement Comparison in Descending Productivity Order						
State	2020 Spending Per Student Adjusted for Cost of Living	2019 NAEP Composite	Productivity: Cost Per NAEP Point	State	2020 Spending Per Student Adjusted for Cost of Living	2019 NAEP Composite	Productivity: Cost Per NAEP Point
US Average	$16,171	252	$64	Maine	$14,907	251	$59
				South Carolina	$15,212	250	$61
Hawaii	$9,174	246	$37	West Virginia	$14,693	243	$60
Idaho	$9,098	253	$36	Montana	$14,645	252	$58
Utah	$10,746	252	$43	Missouri	$14,768	251	$59
Arizona	$10,269	249	$41	Iowa	$16,200	250	$65
Nevada	$11,207	249	$45	Wisconsin	$15,787	252	$63
Florida	$11,503	255	$45	Alaska	$15,696	241	$65
North Carolina	$11,741	251	$47	Nebraska	$16,322	252	$65
California	$11,788	250	$47	Massachusetts	$16,307	256	$64
Mississippi	$13,045	254	$51	Washington	$16,827	253	$67
South Dakota	$12,403	249	$50	Rhode Island	$16,508	249	$66
Oregon	$13,638	252	$54	Michigan	$16,691	249	$67
Oklahoma	$12,283	249	$49	Kansas	$17,563	251	$70
Tennessee	$12,492	246	$51	North Dakota	$17,884	250	$72
Alabama	$13,043	242	$54	Minnesota	$17,960	252	$71
Colorado	$13,882	252	$55	Delaware	$17,469	244	$72
Maryland	$14,441	249	$58	New Hampshire	$17,241	252	$68
Kentucky	$14,341	252	$57	Ohio	$18,577	254	$73
Virginia	$14,098	252	$56	Vermont	$19,883	251	$79
New Mexico	$14,525	247	$59	Connecticut	$19,575	253	$77
Louisiana	$13,828	248	$56	Wyoming	$19,885	253	$78
Georgia	$14,863	253	$59	Illinois	$20,587	251	$82
Arkansas	$13,505	249	$54	New Jersey	$20,560	255	$80
Texas	$15,237	251	$61	Pennsylvania	$20,925	253	$83
Indiana	$14,723	255	$58	New York	$20,602	250	$82

Source: US Census, Missouri Economic Research and Information Center, National Assessment of Educational Progress. NAEP Composite is the 8-score average of 4th Grade and 8th Grade Reading and Math scores for low-income students and all other students, equally weighted. A 10-point difference on NAEP is the equivalent of a year's worth of learning.

Appendix D—State Assessment Results for the Twenty-five Largest Districts

Appendix D - State Assessment Results		All Students/All Grades Tested		2021	
	Math			English language arts		
25 Largest School Districts	Below Grade Level	Grade Level, Needs Remedial Training	On Track for College & Career	Below Grade Level	Grade Level, Needs Remedial Training	On Track for College & Career
Wichita	58%	30%	12%	49%	31%	20%
Olathe	24%	38%	37%	22%	35%	43%
Shawnee Mission	27%	35%	38%	24%	30%	45%
Blue Valley	17%	37%	47%	13%	31%	56%
Kansas City	64%	28%	8%	55%	31%	14%
Topeka	48%	35%	17%	44%	33%	23%
Lawrence	32%	36%	31%	25%	31%	44%
Maize	23%	41%	36%	21%	34%	45%
De Soto	13%	38%	49%	13%	34%	53%
Geary County	30%	37%	33%	26%	35%	38%
Garden City	46%	36%	17%	40%	38%	22%
Derby	32%	39%	29%	30%	35%	35%
Dodge City	45%	37%	18%	46%	34%	20%
Salina	39%	40%	21%	34%	36%	30%
Manhattan-Ogden	26%	35%	39%	21%	33%	46%
Andover	16%	38%	46%	15%	32%	53%
Goddard	23%	39%	38%	20%	33%	46%
Auburn Washburn	26%	40%	34%	22%	36%	42%
Gardner-Edgerton	29%	40%	32%	27%	36%	37%
Haysville	43%	38%	18%	33%	38%	29%
Spring Hill	23%	37%	40%	21%	33%	47%
Liberal	60%	32%	7%	54%	33%	14%
Emporia	45%	36%	19%	33%	37%	29%
Hutchinson	46%	39%	15%	41%	35%	24%
Turner-KC	46%	38%	15%	43%	35%	22%
Source: Kansas Dept. of Education; may not sum to 100% due to rounding						

Endnotes

Introduction

1. Shawnee Mission School District, "Diversity and Equity." Accessed February 17, 2022, https://msd.org/families/diversity-and-equity,
2. Kansas Department of Education, "Kansas Report Card 2020–2021," https://ksreportcard.ksde.org/assessment_results.aspx?org_no=State&rptType=3.
3. Kansas Department of Education, "Kansas Report Card 2020–2021." The Kansas Department of Education defines low-income students as those eligible for free or reduced lunch.
4. Author's calculation of the cumulative difference between at-risk funding in the 2005 school year and that provided in the 2021 school year.
5. Dorsey, David, "At-Risk Funding: Increased Money Fails to Increase Achievement," November 1, 2015, https://kansaspolicy.org//wp-content/uploads/2015/12/KPI-Paper-At-Risk-Funding-Increased-Money-Fails-to-Increase-Achievement.pdf.
6. Kansas Legislative Division of Post Audit, "K–12 Education: Evaluating At-Risk Student Counts, Weights, and Expenditures," December 2019, kslpa.org/audit-report-library/k-12-education-evaluating-at-risk-student-counts-weights-and-expenditures/.
7. Kansas Association of School Boards, "Comparing Kansas 2019: Kansas Still Ranked 9th in Student Outcomes." Accessed February 17, 2022, https://files.eric.ed.gov/fulltext/ED600013.pdf.
8. Kansas Department of Education, "Kansas Report Card 2020–2021."
9. *Giving Kids a Fighting Chance*, Kansas Policy Institute, November 2019, youtube.com/watch?v=WCFwMz_0RrY.
10. U. S. Department of Education, "National Assessment of Educational Progress," comparing 1998 and 2019 performance, nationsreportcard.gov/ndecore/landing.
11. Kansas Chamber of Commerce, "Vision 2025." Accessed February 18, 2022, http://ksvision2025.com/grow-talent-supply.
12. EnterpriseKC, "Establishing Kansas as a Cybersecurity Center of Excellence," December 15, 2020. Copy in author's possession.

Chapter 1

13. Wikipedia, *The Emperor's New Clothes*. Accessed February 18, 2022, https://en.wikipedia.org/wiki/The_Emperor%27s_New_Clothes.
14. Neuenswander, Brad, Kansas Department of Education, November 30 written testimony to the Special Committee on Education. Accessed February 28, 2022, http://www.kslegislature.org/li/b2021_22/committees/misc/ksdetestimonymeasurestudentsuccess.pdf.
15. Kansas Department of Education website. Accessed February 18, 2022, ksde.org.
16. Williams, Walter, "There's academic fraud at every level of education, "*The Winchester Star*, April 24, 2018, winchesterstar.com/opinions/columns/walter-williams-there-s-academic-fraud-at-every-level-of-education/article_146b5e54-1219-517f-bbfe-a14b709695bb.html.
17. Kansas Department of Education, "2021 Academically Prepared for Postsecondary Award," https://www.ksde.org/Agency/Fiscal-and-Administrative-Services/Communications-and-Recognition-Programs/Vision-Kansans-Can/Kansans-Can-Star-Recognition/2021-Awards#PH.
18. Trabert, Dave. Personal recount by one of the authors of this book, who serves on the Public Policy and Advocacy Committee of the Overland Park Chamber of Commerce.

19   Kansas Department of Education, Data Central Kansas K-12 Report Generator, Students Approved for Free- or Reduced-Price Lunches - Headcount Enrollment. Accessed May 16, 2022, https://datacentral.ksde.org/report_gen.aspx.

20   Kansas Association of School Boards, "Comparing Kansas 2019: Kansas Still Ranked 9th in Student Outcomes." Accessed February 17, 2022, https://files.eric.ed.gov/fulltext/ED600013.pdf, p.4.

21   Kansas Association of School Boards, "Comparing Kansas 2019," p. 2.

22   Hanushek, Eric, "Does Money Matter After All," Hoover Institution at Stanford University, July 7, 2015, http://hanushek.stanford.edu/opinions/does-money-matter-after-all.

23   King, Jennifer Rice, *Teacher Quality: Understanding the Effectiveness of Teacher Attributes*, Economic Policy Institute, 2003, https://www.epi.org/publication/books_teacher_quality_execsum_intro/#:~:text=Their%20research%20identifies%20teacher%20quality,important%20predictor%20is%20teacher%20quality.

24   Data reported annually by the Kansas Department of Education to the National Center for Education Statistics and the Consumer Price Index as reported by the U.S. Department of Labor, as calculated by Dr. Benjamin Scafidi.

25   ACT website, act.org/content/act/en/products-and-services/the-act-postsecondary-professionals/scores.html#:~:text=ACT%20College%20Readiness%20Benchmarks,-The%20ACT%20College&text=Students%20who%20meet%20a%20benchmark,corresponding%20college%20course%20or%20courses.

26   Neuenswander, Brad, Kansas Department of Education, testimony before the Special Committee on Education, November 30, 2021, youtube.com/watch?v=O1Dk8hJPs-Q&t=6145s.

27   Kennesaw State University Faculty website, https://facultyweb.kennesaw.edu/bscafidi/index.php.

28   Missouri Economic Research and Information Center, https://meric.mo.gov/.

29   U.S. Census, "2019 Public Elementary-Secondary Education Finance Data," per-student spending is total spending divided by headcount enrollment, www.census.gov/data/tables/2019/econ/school-finances/secondary-education-finance.html; NAEP Data Explorer, www.nationsreportcard.gov/ndecore/landing.

30   Trabert, Dave, "Kansas is #38 for educational bang for the buck," Kansas Policy Institute, June 21, 2021, https://kansaspolicy.org/kansas-is-38-in-bang-for-the-educational-buck.

31   Kufield, Megan, Jim Soland, Karyn Lewis, Emily Morton, "The pandemic has had devastating impacts on learning. What will it take to help students catch up?," Brookings, March 3, 2022, https://www.brookings.edu/blog/brown-center-chalkboard/2022/03/03/the-pandemic-has-had-devastating-impacts-on-learning-what-will-it-take-to-help-students-catch-up.

32   Burns, Emily, Josh Stevenson, Phil Kerpen, "No, masks don't help keep kids in school," EmilyBurns.subsack.com, March 28, 2022. Accessed April 4, 2022, https://emilyburns.substack.com/p/no-masks-dont-help-keep-kids-in-school?s=w.

33   Kansas Department of Education, "Revised State Template for the Consolidated State Plan," March 2017. ksde.org/Portals/0/ECSETS/ESEA/KSconsolidatedstateplan01182018_Approved.pdf.

34   Loveless, Tom, "The NAEP proficiency myth," Brookings Institute, June 13, 2016, https://www.brookings.edu/blog/brown-center-chalkboard/2016/06/13/the-naep-proficiency-myth.

35   Dorsey, David, "At-Risk Funding: Increased Money Fails to Increase Achievement," Kansas Policy Institute, November 2015, https://kansaspolicy.org/kpi-paper-at-risk-funding-increased-money-fails-to-increase-achievement/ and https://kansaspolicy.org/the-time-is-now-to-overhaul-the-k-12-at-risk-program.

36   Trabert, Dave, "Schools ignore legal requirement to conduct needs assessment," *The Sentinel*, November 29, 2021, https://sentinelksmo.org/schools-ignore-legal-requirement-to-conduct-needs-assessments.

Chapter 2

37 Neuenswander, Brad, Kansas Department of Education, email exchange with Dave Trabert, copy in author's possession.

38 Trabert, Dave, "More student achievement deception in Gardner-Edgerton," *The Sentinel*, September 27, 2021, https://sentinelksmo.org/more-student-achievement-deception-in-gardner-edgerton/. The link to Brandon Parks' Facebook comment is no longer active.

39 Neuenswander, Brad, email exchange between Neuenswander and a parent, dated September 25, 2021. Copy in author's possession.

40 Kansas Department of Education, "Kansans Can Star Recognition Program." Accessed February 28, 2022, https://www.ksde.org/Agency/Fiscal-and-Administrative-Services/Communications-and-Recognition-Programs/Vision-Kansans-Can/Kansans-Can-Star-Recognition/Quantitative-Measures/Academically-prepared-for-postsecondary.

41 Kansas Department of Education, "Revised State Template for the Consolidated State Plan," January 8, 2018. https://www.ksde.org/Portals/0/ECSETS/ESEA/KSconsolidatedstateplan01182018_Approved.pdf

42 Email correspondence between Neuenswander and the author.

43 Keillor, Garrison, "A Prairie Home Companion," https://www.prairiehome.org/index.html.

44 Rothman, Robert, "Normed Tests Skewed to Find Most Pupils 'Above Average,' a Disputed Study Finds," EducationWeek, December 9, 1987, https://www.edweek.org/education/normed-tests-skewed-to-find-most-pupils-above-average-a-disputed-study-finds/1987/12.

45 "Comparing Kansas: Educational rankings place Kansas in the top 10," Kansas Association of School Boards, July 22, 2022. https://www.kasb.org/45132?articleID=110515&utm_source=All+KASB+Contacts&utm_campaign=f7d2f3439b-Highlights+July+20%2C+2022&utm_medium=email&utm_term=0_f37074fe94-f7d2f3439b-216195873

46 Neuenswander, Brad, email exchange between Neuenswander and a parent, dated September 25, 2021. Copy in author's possession.

47 Baumgarner, Molly, Senate Education Committee hearing, February 10, 2022. http://sg001-harmony.sliq.net/00287/Harmony/en/PowerBrowser/PowerBrowserV2/20220210/-1/14332

48 Kansas House K–12 Budget Committee hearing, video recording, February 11, 2021, https://www.youtube.com/watch?v=vq9pej59qmQ.

49 Kansas House K–12 Budget Committee hearing.

50 "Mapping State Proficiency Standards," National Center for Education Statistics, https://nces.ed.gov/nationsreportcard/studies/statemapping/

51 "Grades 9-10 Reading: Literature," Kansas Standards for English Language Arts, adopted November 2017, https://community.ksde.org/LinkClick.aspx?fileticket=g4s0HZxjYF4%3d&tabid=5559&mid=13575.

52 U. S. Department of Education, "National Assessment of Educational Progress," 2003 results, nationsreportcard.gov/ndecore/landing.

53 Porter, Jim, biography, https://www.ksde.org/Board/Kansas-State-Board-of-Education/District-9.

54 Porter, Jim, "Kansas citizens deserve to know the whole story about education funding," *Wyandotte Daily*, May 9, 2016, http://www.wyandottedaily.com/guest-column-kansas-citizens-deserve-to-know-the-whole-story-about-education-funding/.

55 Copy of email in author's possession.

56 Copy of email in author's possession.

57 Another school funding lawsuit, *Montoy v. State of Kansas*, was litigated between 1999 and 2006.

58 O'Neal, Mike, "*Gannon*: The Fallacy of the Court's Emerson Analysis," Kansas Policy Institute, April 2017, https://kansaspolicy.org//wp-content/uploads/2017/04/KPI-PB-Gannon-1.pdf

59 Dorsey, David, "Judicial panel used cherry-picked data in *Gannon* decision," Kansas Policy Institute, January 26, 2015, https://kansaspolicy.org/judicial-panel-used-cherry-picked-data-in-gannon-decision.

60 *Staff Notebook*, Kansas City, Kansas, Public Schools, March 22, 2012, https://kansaspolicy.org//wp-content/uploads/2016/01/kcks-newsletter-w-lane-quote.pdf.

61 Williams, Mara Rose, "Kansas City, Kan., school district lays off 31 staff members and cuts pay for 850 others," *Kansas City Star*, May 29, 2015, https://www.kansascity.com/news/article22640394.html.

62 Trabert, Dave, "USD 500 Kansas City misleads on school funding and budget claims," Kansas Policy Institute, June 4, 2015. https://kansaspolicy.org/1090-2/

63 Copy of email in author's possession.

64 "A–F Grading of Kansas Schools," Kansas Policy Institute, https://kansaspolicy.org/a-f.

65 "A–F Grading of Kansas Schools."

66 Trabert, Dave, "Schools ignore legal requirement to conduct needs assessments," *The Sentinel*, November 29, 2021, https://sentinelksmo.org/schools-ignore-legal-requirement-to-conduct-needs-assessments.

67 Kansas Supreme Court, *Ganon IV*, March 2017. https://sentinelksmo.org/wp-content/uploads/2021/10/Gannon-4-March-2017.pdf

68 Copies of emails and read receipts for each superintendent in author's possession.

69 Copy of email in author's possession.

70 Copy of email in author's possession.

71 Kansas State School Board, video recording of the November 9, 2021, meeting, https://www.youtube.com/watch?v=i_oQvzDc3Jo.

Chapter 3

72 Special Committee on Education, Kansas Legislature, December 1, 2021, https://www.youtube.com/watch?v=Njp4q_hMJPY&t=2135s.

73 Trabert, Dave, "KC Star denies CRT in schools, OK with shaming children," *The Sentinel*, October 29, 2021, https://sentinelksmo.org/kc-star-denies-crt-in-schools-ok-with-shaming-children.

74 Clark, Chrissy, "Progressive 'Equity' Group Trains Kansas Teachers To The Tune of $400,000," *The Daily Wire*, July 23, 2021, https://www.dailywire.com/news/progressive-equity-group-trains-kansas-teachers-to-the-tune-of-400000.

75 Trabert, Dave, "More disclosure of SMSD's Deep Equity/CRT indoctrination," *The Sentinel*, July 26, 2021, https://sentinelksmo.org/more-disclosure-of-smsds-deep-equity-crt-indoctrination.

76 Richardson, Patrick, "Critical race theory found in Hiawatha school district," *The Sentinel*, August 11, 2021, https://sentinelksmo.org/critical-race-theory-found-in-hiawatha-school-district.

77 Hiawatha School Board of Education meeting, July 12, 2021. https://www.youtube.com/watch?v=9DPEQ5EZj8Y&t=1821s

78 Kansas Vision for Education, Kansas Department of Education. Accessed March 6, 2022, https://www.ksde.org/Agency/Division-of-Learning-Services/Teacher-Licensure-and-Accreditation/KESA.

79 Board meeting materials for 2022. Accessed March 9, 2022, https://www.ksde.org/Board/Kansas-State-Board-of-Education/Agendas-Meeting-Dates-and-Minutes/2022-Meeting-Materials-Minutes; 2021 Board meeting materials. Accessed the same day, https://www.ksde.org/Board/Kansas-State-Board-of-Education/Agendas-Meeting-Dates-and-Minutes/2021-Meeting-Materials-Minutes.

80 Copies in author's possession.

81 Postsecondary Success, Kansas Department of Education. Accessed March 8, 2022, https://www.ksde.org/Agency/Fiscal-and-Administrative-Services/Communications-and-Recognition-Programs/Vision-Kansans-Can/Kansans-Can-Star-Recognition/Quantitative-Measures/Postsecondary-Success.

82 "Kansas Can Success Tour 2021," Kansas Department of Education, PowerPoint presentation, copy in author's possession.

83 Academically Prepared for Postsecondary, Kansas Department of Education. Accessed March 9, 2022, https://www.ksde.org/Agency/Fiscal-and-Administrative-Services/Communications-and-Recognition-Programs/Vision-Kansans-Can/Kansans-Can-Star-Recognition/Quantitative-Measures/Academically-prepared-for-postsecondary.

84 Steinmeyer, Jim, AZ Quotes, https://www.azquotes.com/author/42601-Jim_Steinmeyer.

85 Education Week, "Summary of the Improving America's Schools Act," November 9, 1994, https://www.edweek.org/education/summary-of-the-improving-americas-schools-act/1994/11.

86 "Pres. Clinton Signing the Improving America's Schools Act of 1994," YouTube, https://www.youtube.com/watch?v=CtvnUHOkRzA.

87 "No Child Left Behind Act," Ballotpedia, https://ballotpedia.org/No_Child_Left_Behind_Act.

88 Trabert, Dave, and Todd Davidson, "Removing Barriers to Better Public Education: Analyzing the facts about student achievement and school spending," Kansas Policy Institute, June 2012, https://kansaspolicy.org/removing-barriers-to-better-public-education-june-2012-update.

89 Email received May 1, 2012, from Kansas Commissioner of Education, Dr. Diane DeBacker, copy in author's possession.

90 Email in author's possession.

91 "Tax Credit for Low Income Students Scholarship Program Legislative Report for January 2022," Kansas Department of Education. Accessed March 11, 2022, https://www.ksde.org/Portals/0/School%20Finance/Action%20Items/Legislative%20Report%20January%202022%20TCLISSP.pdf?ver=2022-01-10-104033-877.

92 "Kansas Can Success Tour 2021", Kansas Department of Education, PowerPoint presentation, copy in author's possession.

93 "Kansas Vision for Education," Kansas Department of Education. Accessed March 13, 2022, https://www.ksde.org/Agency/Fiscal-and-Administrative-Services/Communications-and-Recognition-Programs/Vision-Kansans-Can.

94 Dorsey, David, "Kansans Can – rearranging deck chairs in the name of reform – Part 1," Kansas Policy Institute, https://kansaspolicy.org/kansas-can-rearranging-deck-chairs-name-reform-part-1/.

95 Dorsey, David, "The wrong stuff – new school redesign project should be deep spaced," Kansas Policy Institute, August 11, 2017, https://kansaspolicy.org/wrong-stuff-new-school-redesign-project-deep-spaced/.

96 Watson's quote was from a video that has since been removed by KSDE.

97 "Kansans Can School Redesign Project," Kansas Department of Education. Accessed March 14, 2022, https://www.ksde.org/Agency/Fiscal-and-Administrative-Services/Communications-and-Recognition-Programs/Vision-Kansans-Can/Kansans-Can-School-Redesign-Project.

98 "Accreditation K–12," Kansas Department of Education. Accessed March 14, 2022, https://www.ksde.org/Agency/Division-of-Learning-Services/Teacher-Licensure-and-Accreditation/Accreditation-K-12-Home.

99 "Kansas Education Systems Accreditation 2021-22 Legislative Update," Kansas Department of Education, January 14, 2022, http://www.kslegislature.org/li/b2021_22/committees/misc/kesa20212022legislativeupdate.pdf.

100 "Accreditation Criteria," Kansas Department of Education. Accessed March 14, 2022, https://www.ksde.org/Portals/0/TLA/Accreditation/Accreditation%20Criteria%20-%20Finalr16.pdf?ver=2019-12-18-153701-107.

101 "Board materials, January 2021 meeting of the Kansas Board of Education. Accessed March 14, 2022, https://www.ksde.org/LinkClick.aspx?fileticket=4X5Xnekg2-k%3d&portalid=0.

102 Munger, Charlie, AZquotes. https://www.azquotes.com/quote/1388572.

103 Hicks, David, "Olathe rewards superintendent Yeager for DEI, not academic improvement," *The Sentinel*, May 18, 2022, https://sentinelksmo.org/olathe-rewards-superintendent-yeager-for-dei-not-academic-improvement/.

104 "Strategic Plan 2021-2026," Olathe Public Schools. Accessed May 19, 2022, at https://www.olatheschools.org/cms/lib/KS01907024/Centricity/Domain/2941/Strategic-Plan-040422.pdf.

105 "Strategic Plan Academic Bold Goals," Olathe Public Schools. Accessed May 19, 2022, at https://www.olatheschools.org/cms/lib/KS01907024/Centricity/Domain/2941/Balanced-Scorecard-021622.pdf.

106 Kansas Department of Education, "Revised State Template for the Consolidated State Plan," January 8, 2018. https://www.ksde.org/Portals/0/ECSETS/ESEA/KSconsolidatedstateplan01182018 Approved.pdf.

107 "Evaluating the Need for Developmental Education Courses," Kansas Legislative Division of Post Audit, March 2022, https://www.kslpa.org/audit-report-library/evaluating-the-need-for-developmental-education-courses.

108 High school graduates in 2019 were in the tenth grade in 2017. That year, the state assessment showed 77% of tenth graders needed some degree of remedial training in math, and 71% needed some remedial training in English language arts. https://ksreportcard.ksde.org/assessment results.aspx?org no=State&rptType=3.

109 ACT college readiness report for all states purchased from ACT and received on October 31, 2019. Copy in author's possession.

110 "Meet Your School Board Members," Shawnee Mission School District. Accessed March 16, 2022, https://www.smsd.org/about/board-of-education/meet-your-board-members

111 "Your Board Members," Kansas City Kansas Public Schools. Accessed March 16, 2022, https://kckps.org/about-us/board-of-education/your-board-members.

112 "Representative Stephanie Byers," Kansas State Legislature. Accessed March 16, 2022, http://www.kslegislature.org/li/b2021 22/members/rep byers stephanie 1.

113 "Compliance," Kansas Department of Education. Accessed March 16, 2022, https://www.ksde.org/Portals/0/TLA/Accreditation/Accreditation%20Model/KESA%20COMPLIANCE%20-%20FALL%202017.pdf.

Chapter 4

114 "Kansas School Finance System," Kansas Legislative Research Department, January 18, 2019. Accessed March 17, 2022, http://www.kslegislature.org/KLRD-web/Publications/Education/2019-School-Finance-System-Overview.pdf.

115 "K-12 Education: Evaluating At-Risk Student Counts, Weights, and Expenditures," Kansas Legislative Division of Post Audit, December 2019, https://www.kslpa.org/audit-report-library/k-12-education-evaluating-at-risk-student-counts-weights-and-expenditures/.

116 *Kansas City Star* editorial board, "Why are Kansas schools diverting urgently needed funds from at-risk students?," December 18, 2019, https://www.kansascity.com/opinion/readers-opinion/guest-commentary/article238722248.html.

117 Dorsey, David, "At-Risk Funding: Increased Money Fails to Increase Achievement," Kansas Policy Institute, November 2015, https://kansaspolicy.org/kpi-paper-at-risk-funding-increased-money-fails-to-increase-achievement/.

118 K.S.A. 72-1163(a), http://www.kslegislature.org/li/b2021 22/statute/072 000 0000 chapter/072 011 0000 article/072 011 0063 section/072 011 0063 k/.

119 Kansas Supreme Court, *Ganon IV*, March 2017. https://sentinelksmo.org/wp-content/uploads/2021/10/Gannon-4-March-2017.pdf

120 K.S.A. 72-1163(a), http://www.kslegislature.org/li/b2021 22/statute/072 000 0000 chapter/072 011 0000 article/072 011 0063 section/072 011 0063 k/.

121 Copies of the Coffeyville reports in author's possession and available at https://sentinelksmo.org/wp-content/uploads/2022/05/Coffeyville-combined.pdf; answers compared to percentage of students in Levels 1 and 2 on the state assessment at https://ksreportcard.ksde.org/assessment results.aspx?org no=State&rptType=3.

122 Copies of Roosevelt Middle School and Field Kindley High School reports in author's possession; answers compared to percentage of students in Levels 1 and 2 on the state assessment at https://ksreportcard.ksde.org/assessment_results.aspx?org_no=State&rptType=3.

123 Copies of reports in author's possession.

124 F.L. Schlagle report at https://sentinelksmo.org/wp-content/uploads/2022/05/KCK-Schlagle-Building-Needs-Assessment-FY22-Sheet1-copy.pdf, answers compared to percentage of students in Levels 1 and 2 on the state assessment at https://ksreportcard.ksde.org/assessment_results.aspx?org_no=State&rptType=3.

125 Copies of Schlagle reports in author's possession.

126 Recorded interview with Garry Sigle; copy in author's possession.

127 Senate Bill No. 362, Kansas State Legislature, Session of 2022, http://www.kslegislature.org/li/b2021_22/measures/sb362/.

128 Tallman, Mark, speaking at the February 10, 2022 Senate Education Committee hearing. https://www.youtube.com/watch?v=oPllKuU2xww&t=2550s

129 "Governor's Commission on Racial Equity & Justice: 2021 Report," Kansas Governor's Office, December 2021, https://governor.kansas.gov/wp-content/uploads/2022/02/CREJ-Report-December-2021_FINAL_Print.pdf.

130 "Governor's Council on Tax Reform," Kansas Governor's Office, January 2020. Accessed April 4, 2022, https://governor.kansas.gov/wp-content/uploads/2020/01/Revenue-Tax-Council-Report-Rev.-012220.pdf.

131 Evans, Ganon, "What is the government's fair share of what you earn?" Kansas Policy Institute, October 29, 2021, https://kansaspolicy.org/what-is-the-governments-fair-share-of-what-you-earn/.

132 Stegall, Caleb, "A Kansas Primer on Education Funding, Volume II: Analysis of *Montoy vs. State of Kansas*," Kansas Policy Institute, 2009, https://kansaspolicy.org/volume-ii-analysis-of-montoy-vs-state-of-kansas/.

133 Stegall, "A Kansas Primer on Education Funding."

134 Stegall, "A Kansas Primer on Education Funding."

135 O'Neal, Mike, "Reaction to Kansas Supreme Court Ruling on *Gannon* School Finance Case," Kansas Policy Institute, March 10, 2014, https://kansaspolicy.org/2223-2/.

136 Kansas Constitution, Article 6, Section 6(b), https://kslib.info/832/Article-6-Education.

137 Kansas Constitution, Article 2, Section 24, https://kslib.info/828/Article-2-Legislative.

138 Kansas Statute, Article 72-64c01(a), http://www.kslegislature.org/li_2012/b2011_12/statute/072_000_0000_chapter/072_064c_0000_article/072_064c_0001_section/072_064c_0001_k/.

139 "Accounting Handbook," Kansas Department of Education. Accessed March 18, 2022, https://www.ksde.org/Portals/0/School%20Finance/guidelines_manuals/Accounting%20Handbook18.pdf?ver=2021-12-01-082356-430.

140 "Accounting Handbook," Kansas Department of Education.

141 Author's calculation of data compiled from Kansas Department of Education's Comparative Performance and Fiscal System, https://datacentral.ksde.org/cpfs.aspx.

142 Author's calculations; change in Consumer Price Index for Midwest cities on a fiscal-year basis, https://www.bls.gov/cpi/.

Chapter 5

143 "History of the Education Article of the Constitution of the State of Kansas," Kansas Office of the Revisor of Statutes, December 19, 2017, http://www.kslegislature.org/li_2018/b2017_18/committees/ctte_spc_2017_special_comp_resp_school_finance_1/documents/testimony/20171219_01.pdf.

144 Scudella, Vincent, "State Education Governance Models," Education Commission of the States, August 2013, https://www.ecs.org/clearinghouse/01/08/70/10870.pdf.

145 Sowell, Thomas, *Dismantling America*, Basic Books, August 2010, https://www.goodreads.com/quotes/1296215-no-one-will-really-understand-politics-until-they-understand-that.

146 Dorsey, David, "Proposed $900 million K–12 funding increase displays State Board's disconnection and dysfunction," Kansas Policy Institute, August 2, 2016, https://kansaspolicy.org/proposed-900-million-k-12-funding-increase-displays-state-boards-disconnection-dysfunction/.

147 Kansas State Board of Education Meeting video, Kansas Department of Education, July 12, 2016, https://www.youtube.com/watch?v=wFmyp-ao4uw.

148 Dorsey, David, "Proposed $900 million K–12 funding increase."

149 "Total Expenditures Report," KSDE Data Central, School Finance Reports, Kansas Department of Education. https://datacentral.ksde.org/school_finance_reports.aspx.

150 Ryan, Michael, "Who is the gatekeeper to your child's mind? Lawmakers versus the education board," *Kansas City Star*, July 1, 2021, https://www.kansascity.com/opinion/opn-columns-blogs/michael-ryan/article252477893.html.

151 Kansas State Board of Education Meeting video, Kansas Department of Education, June 9, 2021. https://www.youtube.com/watch?v=E4br9oWxl-Q.

152 Dorsey, David, "Proposed $900 million K–12 funding increase."

153 Recorded interview with Kristey Williams, copy in author's possession.

154 Recorded interview with Mike O'Neal, copy in author's possession.

155 Recorded interview with Kristey Williams, copy in author's possession.

156 Recorded interview with Kristey Williams, copy in author's possession.

157 Recorded interview with Mike O'Neal, copy in author's possession.

158 Recorded interview with Mike O'Neal, copy in author's possession.

159 Recorded interview with Douglas Shane, copy in author's possession.

160 Recorded interview with Douglas Shane, copy in author's possession.

161 "Public Participation at Board Meetings," Manhattan-Ogden School District. Accessed May 17, 2022, at https://www.usd383.org/home/showpublisheddocument/24844/637211815614730000.

162 "How to Address the Board," Kansas City, Kansas, Public Schools, https://go.boarddocs.com/ks/kckps/Board.nsf/vpublic?open.

163 "SMSD Board Meeting," August 23, 2021, https://www.youtube.com/watch?v=T9pfyxjcwDM&list=PLIUE_HxtdiNPl909f4YFpftuY8foJkkqO&index=16&t=385s.

164 Shipley, Rebecca, transcript and private recording of her remarks, May 5, 2022, https://www.facebook.com/1480957202/posts/10227754194388605/?d=n.

165 Trabert, Dave, "Taxpayer exposes Olathe school board president's bullying, misinformation tactics," *The Sentinel*, May 23, 2022, https://sentinelksmo.org/taxpayer-exposes-olathe-school-board-presidents-bullying-misinformation-tactics/.

166 Urban Preparatory Academy, http://www.upacademywichita.org/about-up/.

167 Perez, Suzanne Tobias, "Urban Preparatory Academy of Wichita to serve kindergarten through fifth grade," *Wichita Eagle*, March 27, 2014, https://www.kansas.com/news/article1138530.html

168 Perez, "Urban Preparatory Academy of Wichita."

169 "2017 Legal Max," Kansas Department of Education, accessed May 19, 2022, at https://www.ksde.org/Agency/Fiscal-and-Administrative-Services/School-Finance/Legal-Max-General-Fund-School-Finance-Studies/ItemId/4120; $9,324 is the average aid flowing through the district's General Fund and Local Option Budget.

170 "Comparative Performance and Fiscal System," Kansas Department of Education, data downloaded and tabulated against KSDE enrollment report for 2017. Copy in author's possession.

171 Perez, Suzanne Tobias, "Wichita district says no to new schools in old schools," *Wichita Eagle*, May 9, 2017, https://www.kansas.com/article149434384.html.

172 Perez, "Wichita district says no to new schools."

173 Phillips Fundamental Learning Center, https://www.funlearn.org/.

174 "Dyslexia FAQ," The Yale Center for Dyslexia & Creativity, accessed June 9, 2022, at https://dyslexia.yale.edu/dyslexia/dyslexia-faq/#:~:text=Dyslexia%20affects%2020%20percent%20of,brightest%20children%20struggle%20to%20read.

175 Written statement provided by Roger Lowe; copy in author's possession.

176 Email exchange with Roger Lowe, copy in author's possession.
177 Kansas Department of Education, 2021 state assessment results, https://ksreportcard.ksde.org/assessment_results.aspx?org_no=State&rptType=3.
178 "Jerry Pournelle," Wikipedia, https://en.wikipedia.org/wiki/Jerry_Pournelle#:~:text=Another%20%22law%22%20of%20his%20is,and%20sometimes%20are%20eliminated%20entirely.
179 Pournelle, Jerry, "Chaos Manor Special Reports," September 10, 2010, https://www.jerrypournelle.com/reports/jerryp/iron.html.
180 Recorded interview with David Dorsey, copy in author's possession.
181 Recorded interview with David Dorsey.
182 Recorded interview with Kathy Martin, copy in author's possession.
183 Lowenstein, Roger, "Massachusetts May Take Control of Boston's Public Schools," *Wall Street Journal*, April 22, 2022, https://www.wsj.com/articles/massachusetts-take-control-boston-public-schools-underperforming-education-enrollment-achievement-gap-school-choice-remote-learning-charters-pilot-11650653168.
184 "*USD NO. 229 v. State of Kansas*," December 2, 1994, https://law.justia.com/cases/kansas/supreme-court/1994/70-931-3.html.
185 Constitution of the State of Kansas, https://www.kssos.org/other/pubs/KS_Constitution.pdf.
186 Stegall, Caleb, "A Kansas Primer on Education Funding, Volume II: Analysis of Montoy vs. State of Kansas," Kansas Policy Institute, 2009, https://kansaspolicy.org/volume-ii-analysis-of-montoy-vs-state-of-kansas/.
187 Stegall, Caleb, "A Kansas Primer."

Chapter 6

188 Trabert, Dave, "Kansas is #38 for educational bang for the buck," Kansas Policy Institute, June 21, 2021, https://kansaspolicy.org/kansas-is-38-in-bang-for-the-educational-buck.
189 *Giving Kids a Fighting Chance*, Kansas Policy Institute, November 2019, https://www.youtube.com/watch?v=WCFwMz_0RrY&feature=youtu.be.
190 "School choice in Florida," EdChoice. Accessed March 21, 2022, https://www.edchoice.org/school-choice/state/florida/.
191 *Giving Kids a Fighting Chance*, Kansas Policy Institute.
192 *Giving Kids a Fighting Chance*, Kansas Policy Institute.
193 "Charter Schools," Kansas Department of Education, https://www.ksde.org/Agency/Division-of-Learning-Services/Career-Standards-and-Assessment-Services/CSAS-Home/Graduation-and-Schools-of-Choice/Charter-Schools.
194 "Second Conference Committee Report Brief, Senate Substitute for House Bill No. 2567," Kansas Legislature, April 27, 2022, http://www.kslegislature.org/li/b2021_22/measures/documents/ccrb_hb2567_02_042722.pdf.
195 "Testimony: HB 2553," Dr. Tonya Merrigan, USD 229 Blue Valley Schools and Dr. Brent Yeager, Olathe Public Schools USD 233, February 1, 2022, http://www.kslegislature.org/li/b2021_22/committees/ctte_h_k12_education_budget_1/documents/testimony/20220201_115.pdf.
196 "Testimony: HB 2553."
197 "Testimony: HB 2553."
198 "Total Expenditures 2021," Kansas Department of Education, Data Central. Accessed March 22, 2022, https://datacentral.ksde.org/school_finance_reports.aspx.
199 "Open enrollment bill receives criticism from Kansas school districts, Board of Education," KSHB-TV, February 10, 2022, https://www.kshb.com/news/local-news/open-enrollment-bill-receives-criticism-from-kansas-school-districts-board-of-education.
200 Bramhall, Emily, "Why Does Segregation between School Districts Matter for Educational Equity,?" Housing Matters, May 12, 2021, https://housingmatters.urban.org/articles/why-does-segregation-between-school-districts-matter-educational-equity.

201 "Dividing Lines: How School Districts Draw Attendance Boundaries to Perpetuate School Segregation," Urban Institute, September 14, 2021, https://apps.urban.org/features/dividing-lines-school-segregation/.

202 Dorsey, David, "National study's evidence of structural segregation in public education also true in Kansas," Kansas Policy Institute, November 28, 2021, https://kansaspolicy.org/national-studys-evidence-of-structural-segregation-in-public-education-also-true-in-kansas/.

203 Recorded interview with Mike O'Neal, copy in author's possession.

204 "House Chamber Proceedings Part 1 of 2," Kansas Legislature, April 28, 2022, https://www.youtube.com/watch?v=4ub1Yka8PUI.

205 Smith, Aaron Garth, "Open Enrollment Provides Substantial Benefits to Students and Families," Reason Foundation, January 28, 2020, https://reason.org/commentary/open-enrollment-provides-substantial-benefits-to-students-and-families/#:~:text=Black%2C%20low%2Dincome%2C%20and,participants%20to%20exit%20the%20program.

206 Taylor, Mac, "Evaluation of the School District of Choice Program," January 27, 2016, https://lao.ca.gov/Publications/Report/3331.

207 "Testimony: HB 2553."

208 Ditch, Linda, "Former Hayden administrator writes book about career in education," *Topeka Capital-Journal*, June 2, 2019, https://www.cjonline.com/story/news/education/2019/06/02/former-hayden-administrator-writes-book-about-career-in-education/5006161007/.

209 "Senate Chamber Proceedings Part 1 of 2," Kansas Legislature, April 28, 2022, https://www.youtube.com/watch?v=rfThxxYDl3Y.

210 "Senate Chamber Proceedings Part 1 of 2."

211 Gannon, Rebecca, "Open enrollment will allow Kansas students to enroll in any school district," KMBC News, May 2, 2022, https://www.kmbc.com/article/kansas-open-enrollment-will-allow-students-to-enroll-in-any-school-district/39880069.

212 Gannon, Rebecca, "Open enrollment."

213 Trabert, Dave, and Todd Davidson, "Removing Barriers to Better Public Education: Analyzing the facts about student achievement and school spending," Kansas Policy Institute, June 2012, https://kansaspolicy.org/removing-barriers-to-better-public-education-june-2012-update.

214 "Kansas Report Card 2020–21," Kansas Department of Education. Accessed May 25, 2022, at https://ksreportcard.ksde.org/assessment_results.aspx?org_no=State&rptType=3.

215 "2021 School Grades Overview," Florida Department of Education. Accessed March 21, 2022, at https://www.fldoe.org/core/fileparse.php/18534/urlt/SchoolGradesOverview21.pdf.

216 "A-F School Grading," ExcelinEd Policy Toolkit. Accessed March 22, 2022, at https://excelined.org/wp-content/uploads/2020/10/ExcelinEd.PolicyToolkit.AFSchoolGrading.PolicySummary.2018.pdf.

217 "A-F School Grading," ExcelinEd, https://excelined.org/policy-playbook/a-f-school-grading/.

218 "A-F School Grading," ExcelinEd, https://excelined.org/policy-playbook/a-f-school-grading/.

219 "Kansas School Building Report Card," Kansas Policy Institute, https://kansaspolicy.org/a-f/.

220 *Giving Kids a Fighting Chance*, Kansas Policy Institute.

221 HB 2690, Kansas Legislature, http://www.kslegislature.org/li/b2021_22/measures/hb2690/.

222 Kansas Department of Education's list of soft skills includes things like work ethic, teamwork, verbal communications, and ethics/social responsibility. Kansans Can Success Tour PowerPoint presentation, copy in author's possession.

223 "Written Opponent Testimony," Kansas State Board of Education, February 15, 2022, http://www.kslegislature.org/li/b2021_22/committees/ctte_h_k12_education_budget_1/documents/testimony/20220215_01.pdf.

224 "Written Opponent Testimony," Kansas State Board of Education."

225 "Opponent Testimony before the House K–12 Education Budget Committee," Kansas Association of School Boards, February 15, 2022, http://www.kslegislature.org/li/b2021_22/committees/ctte_h_k12_education_budget_1/documents/testimony/20220215_03.pdf.

226 "Written Testimony before the House K–12 Education Budget Committee," Kansas PTA, February 14, 2022, http://www.kslegislature.org/li/ b2021 22/committees/ctte h k12 education budget 1/documents/ testimony/20220215 05.pdf.

227 "Written Testimony," Kansas National Education Association, February 14, 2022, http://www.kslegislature.org/li/b2021 22/committees/ctte h k12 education budget 1/documents/testimony/20220215 06.pdf.

228 "Early Warning! Why Reading by the End of Third Grade Matters," Annie Casey Foundation, January 1, 2010, https://www.aecf.org/resources/ early-warning-why-Reading-by-the-end-of-third-grade-matters.

229 *Giving Kids a Fighting Chance*, Kansas Policy Institute.

230 "Minutes of the February 25, 2013, Senate Education Committee meeting," Kansas Legislature, http://www.kslegislature.org/li 2014/b2013 14/ committees/ctte s ed 1/documents/minutes/20130225.pdf.

231 "Minutes of the February 25, 2013, Senate Education Committee meeting."

232 *Giving Kids a Fighting Chance*, Kansas Policy Institute.

233 *Giving Kids a Fighting Chance*, Kansas Policy Institute.

234 *Giving Kids a Fighting Chance*, Kansas Policy Institute.

235 Scafidi, Ben, "Myths vs. Facts," EdChoice, https://www.edchoice.org/wp- content/uploads/2021/10/Session-5-Myths-vs.-Facts-Dr.-Ben-Scafidi.pdf.

236 McShane, Michael, "The Accountability Myth," EdChoice, September 2021, https://www.edchoice.org/wp-content/uploads/2021/09/The-Accountability- Myth-by-Michael-Q-McShane.pdf.

237 Bedrick, Jason, "Who's Afraid of School Choice," EdChoice, November 23, 2021, https://www.edchoice.org/engage/new-report-whos-afraid-of-school-choice/.

238 Trabert, Dave, "Kansas is #38 for educational bang for the buck," Kansas Policy Institute, June 21, 2021, https://kansaspolicy.org/ kansas-is-38-in-bang-for-the-educational-buck.

239 U.S. Census, "2019 Public Elementary-Secondary Education Finance Data," total spending and headcount enrollment for 2019, https://www.census.gov/data/ tables/2019/econ/school-finances/secondary-education-finance.html; 2020 cost of living factor from Missouri Economic Research and Information Center https://meric.mo.gov/.

240 *Giving Kids a Fighting Chance*, Kansas Policy Institute.

Chapter 7

241 Assumes students not tested (Grades 1, 2, 9, 11, and 12) are proportionately proficient as students in the other grades who participate in the state assessment.

242 *Giving Kids a Fighting Chance*, Kansas Policy Institute, November 2019, youtube.com/watch?v=WCFwMz 0RrY.

243 "The Latest: Brownback advocates school choice, merit pay," AP News, January 10, 2017, https://apnews.com/article/06f3f6e3853c46ab8676873394a9ff2b.

244 "Kansas Schools," Laura Kelly for Kansas. Accessed March 25, 2022, https://www.laurakellyforkansas.com/issues/kansas-schools/.

245 Schopenhauer, Arthur, "Arthur Schopenhauer Quotes," BrainyQuote. Accessed March 28, 2022, https://www.brainyquote.com/authors/ arthur-schopenhauer-quotes.

246 Eakins, Joy, "House Bill 2119 Student Empowerment Action," Kansas Legislature. Accessed March 28, 2022, http://www.kslegislature.org/ li/b2021 22/committees/ctte h k12 education budget 1/documents/ testimony/20210208 08.pdf.

247 Tobias, Suzanne Perez, "Wichita school board member: Don't shut down debate," *Wichita Eagle*, October 25, 2017. Accessed March 28, 2022, https://www.kansas.com/news/local/education/article180806231.html.

248 Weeks, Bob, "Wichita school board meeting: Not for the Public," *Wichita Liberty*, February 29, 2012. Accessed March 28, 2022, https://www.wichitaliberty.org/ wichita-kansas-schools/wichita-school-board-meeting-not-for-the-public/.

249 Kansas State Board of Education, District 8, https://www.ksde.org/Board/ Kansas-State-Board-of-Education/District-8.

250 Recorded interview with David Dorsey.

251 Memmott, Mark, and Korva Coleman, "Michigan Governor Signs Right-to-Work Bills Into Law," National Public Radio, December 11, 2012, https://www.npr.org/sections/thetwo-way/2012/12/11/166946294/michigan-lawmakers-poised-to-pass-right-to-work-bill-outraging-union-protesters.

252 "The Overton Window," Mackinac Center for Public Policy, https://www.mackinac.org/OvertonWindow#faq.

253 Berra, Yogi, "Yogi Berra Quotes," BrainyQuote. Accessed March 28, 2022, https://www.brainyquote.com/quotes/yogi_berra_124868#:~:text=Yogi%20Berra%20Quotes&text=Please%20enable%20Javascript-,You've%20got%20to%20be%20very%20careful%20if%20you%20don,you%20might%20not%20get%20there.

254 *Giving Kids a Fighting Chance*, Kansas Policy Institute.

Made in the USA
Coppell, TX
22 August 2022

81812264R00096